GETTING TO KNOW GOD FOR STRANGERS

DEACON GREGORY HARRIS

Copyright © 2021 Deacon Gregory Harris
All rights reserved
First Edition

PAGE PUBLISHING, INC.
Conneaut Lake, PA

First originally published by Page Publishing 2021

ISBN 978-1-6624-4216-2 (pbk)
ISBN 978-1-6624-4217-9 (digital)

Printed in the United States of America

Thanks to my wife, Linda, my children, and grandchildren. Also, two of my Sunday school students, Clayton and Paul. There will always be a special place in my heart for you and to the countless others whom I do not have room enough to name. I love you all.

In loving memory Georgia Mills Harris

Contents

Prologue 9
Knowledge 17
Faith 27
Stadium versus Church 33
Belief 49
Peace 58
Trust 64
Hope 70
Love 74
Epilogue 83
Index 87
Reference 89
Reference 91

Prologue

There are so many distractions in our society aimed at making us believe that we can look better, or become slimmer, or prettier. We spend billions of dollars each year on products to make our hair thicker, help our nails grow longer, remove wrinkles, and make our skin lighter and clearer so that we can look young again. There are thousands and thousands of workout centers on every continent showing us ways to become shapelier.

Some of us have become obsessed with plastic surgery, even going so far as having our nose and chin broken and reconstructed so that we can look like someone else. Our faces are stretched tightly to clear bags under our eyes, or lines across our forehead. We reshape our bodies through liposuction and bariatric surgery, even though these procedures often require more than one surgery, and the recovery period is lengthy, taking as long as six months for the swelling, numbness, and pain to go away. And we don't care about the danger these procedures pose. We even sign off on forms stating that any errors, or complications will not be the doctor's fault. Then two or three years later, we are confronted with the same dilemma: Do I have this surgery again, or do I go on feeling as depressed as I was before the surgery? We are always looking for ways to alter our appearance when there really is no need to look like anybody but ourselves. We've all had the experience of trying to make ourselves look more attractive to impress someone who, in most cases, is not even interested.

We often follow other people's advice, whether it's right, or wrong. How many times have you thought, *I should not have listened to so-and-so* or *I would not be in this mess if I had listened to myself?* Don't feel bad. We have all done this at one time, or another. The question is when do we stop listening to others and start listening to what's called our first mind—that little voice we hear first but rarely listen to that is usually right. You know, God has never made anything ugly. It's us looking at ourselves that way. We are beautiful people. We have many wonderful qualities that God gave us when we came into the world that we tend to forget about that we have ready at our disposal. We just have to tap into them. There is not a mother who thinks her baby was born ugly. Not one. Remember beauty is in the eye of the beholder. If we are lacking in anything, it's loving our brothers and sisters just as we love ourselves and treating others as we would like to be treated. If you do not read this book all the way through, you can part with this bit of advice. If you do read on, I guarantee you will get caught like I did.

Now let's back up to when we were born into this world. Just like animals have defenses to protect themselves from predators, for example, a porcupine has quills, a skunk has a smell, we have senses that we rely on for survival. We have common sense (and even though it's called common, a lot of us don't use it), and the five senses of sight, smell, hear, taste, and feel. We also have one more sense that is just as important and that is discernment. Yeah, that's the sense you should have followed when maybe you thought you knew what was going to happen, or you felt like you were in danger. Discernment is always there to help us. It was given to us at birth from God.

This book does not focus on the outside your body. It focuses on the inside—the heart. If you work on the inside, the outside will be beautiful without altering it through surgery, or buying expensive products. And the work you do on the inside is everlasting. If you continue to clean the outside a trash can for years and years, how do you suppose the inside will smell? This is a book that will teach you how to tap into your resources that came from the Source. All the things you need are within you regardless of how smart you are, or how much money you have.

A lot of things are going to change in your life. Some things will take a 180-degree turn. You may feel like you are losing because instead of getting one of those quick-fix products to make yourself look pretty on the outside, you will be taking on the challenge of working on the inside. If I were to choose whether to use something that was freely given to me, or to continue to buy products that I will keep having to buy more of with my hard-earned money, well, you figure it out.

Do you think in your wildest dreams that the doctors who perform facial reconstruction do the same thing on their faces just because they have a few wrinkles? It's a different story if a person has been in a terrible accident, or something of that nature, but reconstructive surgery to look younger, well, that's another story. I'm not saying that there is anything wrong with looking younger, but if you think it is supposed to make you feel younger, then maybe you ought to revisit that thought and clarify your objective. Feeling younger has to come from inside, not from looking younger on the outside.

If this is your first attempt at getting in touch with your inner self, getting to know you instead of getting to know someone else, you are at the fork in the road. It is much easier to get to know someone else than it is to get to know yourself. Some people never get to know who they are. It is up to you to decide whether to take the easy road, or to start focusing on the goodness within that will bring out the beauty in you.

This book is the start of a new you. The Source will help you develop an inner strength that you never thought you had. You will say to yourself, "I never thought this way before." It won't be easy at first, but if you hang in there, you will be amazed at the turnaround in your life. Your life will become more meaningful.

Let me tell you a story about the caterpillar. It crawls around on the ground day in and day out. It is in danger all the time from spiders, birds, and other predators. The only thing the caterpillar has is plenty of greens to eat. It suffers while it's in the form of a caterpillar. If it survives long enough to make a cocoon, it has to stay cramped up for what probably seems like forever to the caterpillar. And the caterpillar wonders, *Why have I suffered all my life? I've been cursed for as long as I've been around.* Before long, though, the caterpillar realizes that a change is taking place while it's inside that cocoon. It decides it wants to go on and see what it's going to become. And so the caterpillar gives everything it has to spreading its newly developed wings.

The wings get stronger and stronger until the caterpillar breaks out of its cocoon and emerges as a beautiful butterfly with the prettiest colors you have ever seen. This is an example of God's work.

This book will get you more acquainted with God. I challenge you to read it, or finger through the pages and see how the words come to life. Every sentence and chapter has something you can identify with. I know you are saying, "Not another one of those religious books." I used to say the same thing. This book differs a little from your average book. This is a book that opens the door to a wonderful life with God. Sometimes we are intimidated by the words of religious books, or we find them too boring to read. Perhaps you've thought, *I can't feel whatever I am supposed to feel*, or *I'm just not feeling it*. I understand where you are coming from. I've been right where you are. But I took a leap of faith. I was unhappy with the way my life was going, and I had nowhere to turn, so I tried God. It was the best choice I ever made. My worst day since I came to Jesus is better than my best day when I didn't have Him. So for the last thirty years or so, I have been serving Him. I used to be a very selfish man, but something happened. I can't pinpoint exactly when it was, but little by little, I began to change into this new creature. I am not who I used to be. I cannot hold in this joy I feel on the inside. I will not keep it for myself. I have to share it with my fellow men and women. It is my duty to get this information to you, and I ask you to please bear with me so I may share this knowledge with you and do what has been asked of me.

You are in for a change in your life. Because the content of this book is user-friendly, all you have to do is practice it in your daily life. I know what you are thinking: *This is not the right time. I just got this new boyfriend,* or *new girlfriend, and things aren't as bad as I pretend them to be. I can tolerate my present condition,* or *my new friend can help me weather this storm.* Some will say, "I just got married, or we just had a new baby." Your life may be all right at the present time, and you may feel that it's not the right time. We all know that people don't come to God unless they're going through a perilous time. But there is no better time than now. No matter how good you may think your life is, and I tell you this from experience, that same way you are riding high, there is going to be a low point in your life. You may think you don't need Him on the mountaintop, but when you get into the muddy valley, you are going to need God.

Let's evaluate ourselves a little bit. Did you know any bullies as a kid? They physically and verbally harassed people beginning way back in elementary school, and they have been the same way since. Or what about the guy who was always in competition? Everything he did was competitive, even down to eating lunch in the cafeteria. As these people, or shall I say children, grow up, they carry these traits into adulthood if their behavior is not checked. They will do whatever it takes to tear you down in the workplace, even if it drives you into a depressive state. You get the same feeling you had on the playground in school. You feel as if you can't even do the things that matter to you because they are living in your thoughts. You may excuse it as not being a problem for you, but whether you are a victim, or someone who observes this type of behavior, if you don't do something to stop it, if you condone it, you are just as guilty as the person who is acting that way. Just because it's not happening to us does not make it okay.

And this doesn't just go on in our jobs. We have this problem in our churches. Yes, bullies go to church. And the way to stop them is to check them in the act. We can't act like we don't see it. We are each other's brothers and sisters, and we must act accordingly. There are people in the Body of Christ that get mixed up. They forget that they are serving God, not man. From the playground to the workforce, we must learn to treat each other as we would like to be treated. This is not hard. This book was not written just for people outside the church. It was written for people inside too.

I would like to remind those who have been under a bully's scope of the adage that "sticks and stones may break my bones, but names will never harm me." It may sound corny, but it works. If you know something is not true, then don't sweat it. It really is that simple. Always remember that it's what is on the inside—the content in you—that counts. So do not let outside activity dictate the way you feel. Become sure of yourself and become satisfied with who you are. This is the way. I can give you assurance that if you start to prac-

that's right, start to practice it—your life will never be the same. But you must be true to yourself without the excuses.

One more thing about bullies: They are now spitting their venom on the internet, so we must warn our kids and talk with them in advance so that if they do run into a bully on the internet, it won't have much of an impact on them. This way, our children won't think about harming themselves.

After we've fortified our physical appearance, we start on our next project to make us happy. It's called keeping up with the Joneses. We obsess over who has the biggest house, the nicest clothes, or most expensive car. And feeding this monster can take all that we have: exotic trips, like the father down the block took his family on; buying the big house, like our coworker Tom has; getting the jewelry that your wife's girlfriends have; and buying the most expensive car, like my brother has. It goes on and on until there is more going out than coming in, and you wonder, *How am I going to pay for all the stuff that I have accumulated?* About nine months after you get your fancy car, a new model comes out, and you want that one. We know how that turns out: the same way with the clothes, the house, the new face, and body. It all gets old. Then you start all over trying to get that feeling of newness, or that feeling of euphoria, which fades every time you use, or wear your new items. I'm not saying that we should not have these things. What I'm saying is that we should not depend solely on these things to bring us happiness. These are what we call outside stimuli, and they vanish quickly. We have a bottomless pit in our being, and we try to fill it with all these things from the outside. We can never satisfy the wanting. We never have a sense of fulfillment. Why do we see people buying houses with ten bathrooms? Ask them if they use all the bathrooms and hear what they say. That same person will go and buy a second and third house with as many, or more bathrooms. When does it stop? No matter how much money you have, how much energy you have, you will never fill that bottomless pit. Even those who try to fill it with alcohol, or drugs know it cannot be filled.

The remedy for the bottomless pit syndrome is to ask yourself if you are really happy. I went through this in my own life, and I realized that something had to change. I couldn't keep acting as if everything was okay when it was not. Once I acknowledged that I had a problem, I began on the road to changing my life. Trust me, I tried all the ways you are thinking of trying, but after exhausting all the options that I thought would work, I always came back to God the Father. If you want to take the shortcut to Him, this is your chance right now. Don't go back to being enslaved with that burden of a yoke around your neck. Go forward on this path and see how light your yoke will be. Try your hardest to give yourself over to God for at least three months. What's three months out of your life for the possibility of making it better than you could ever imagine?

Eyes have not seen, ears have not heard, and the heart has not conceived what God has in store for us, His chosen. He chose us way before we got to this point. He already had us in mind. All we have to do is take that first step toward Him, and our life will be changed forever. That's a guarantee. There are not many guarantees in life. Oh, you have warrantees on your appliances and your car, but they will expire. With Him, it is for eternity and that you can take to the bank. Don't take your life as it was so personally. You are not the only one who thought that by trying to fill the pit, it would make you happier. There are people you know at your job, or at church who seem like the perfect family, or the perfect couple. We all struggle to keep everything afloat. You have not failed in this fork of the road. It's what you do from this point on that matters. Do you go with the Father, or do you go back to business as usual? The choice is yours.

To save yourself time and more pain, stop here and think on it because this is one of the most important decisions you will make in your life. It may not be important to you at the moment, but the end result of your choice will let you know whether you were right, or wrong, and if you are wrong, you will wind up right back at the fork in the road. To keep from hearing, "I told you so," go down the road that the Father is on. Trust me, everyone will have this choice to make. You are here now. It didn't just happen by chance that you are at the fork in the road. It was planned so that you could make this choice. It took a lot of time and pain for you to get here. Very wide is the road to destruction, and very narrow and hard to find is the road to eternal life. You are here because of God's grace. You may not understand the significance of this and that's okay. This is going to make a big impact on your life from this point forward.

I must warn you: When and if you go down this fork in the road, you are going to be met with a lot of new challenges some that are going to get you to second-guess this new way of life. Your family and friends are going to see the difference in you immediately, and they are going to talk about you. They may start to dislike you, but this is only going to strengthen you. I'm telling you in advance that you must persevere. Seek out people who also have made this change in their lives and ask them for their support. You will be fragile at the beginning, like a newborn baby, until you begin to trust in God, like you did your parents. And you will become aware of how He begins a new work in you at your weakest point. That is when you will see the power of God. Don't take it personally. Everyone must go through this. Some fall by the wayside and never receive the fullness of His grace, but if you hold on to His unchanging hand, you will see so many miracles in your life. By the way, have you ever witnessed a miracle? Before you answer this question, google the word "miracle" to get the full meaning. Until now, you were experiencing luck. From this point forward, you will experience blessings, and they will flow continually with the renewing of your mind.

As you indulge yourself in the Word and get to know about the Father, your mind will start to renew itself. Remember what I said earlier: *Don't worry about what family and friends say. This is for you, and you have to go down this road alone.* No one can do this for you. But yet you are not alone. You have the Father with you, and He promises to never leave you. He will be with you until the end. The reality is, we all have good days and bad days but that doesn't lessen our responsibility to help one another. When one of us is going through a trial, we must lift them up. We can help them get past the rough days because we have been there. We help one another until we get stronger. This goes for our biological families too.

Knowledge

When we leave our comfort zones for the first time, it's usually around the time we are getting ready to go off to college, or getting our first apartment. We are excited because we are going to live on our own, no more being told what to do, no more curfew, and no one telling us when to get out of bed. The main thing about this move out of our parents' house is that we are going to immediately start to gain some know-how. A person who stays under the guidance of their parents' home will not take the first step toward independence. We are going to learn how to feel comfortable in an uncomfortable situation. We will see that life has all kinds of twists and turns and about faces, and we have to learn to go with the flow. I know that sounds corny, but it's true. We can't control what life brings, but we have some control over how we handle it. Life can be very difficult at the beginning because we don't know what to expect. We were so protected by our parents that we didn't feel the blows that life was giving out when we were at home. We were cushioned by our parents taking the blows on our behalf. As good parents, they never let us feel the anxiety that they were feeling. We were protected. But now that we have moved on to college, or a new apartment, it is all on us. Anxiety starts to creep into our lives. At this point, it helps if you were not too sheltered and, hopefully, learned some coping skills. If not, you will learn quickly.

Some of us feel this new way of life came a little too soon, and it's more than we can handle, so we return home. This is not a sign of failure but a time to regroup and try again. Now we can see how protected we have been. Some of us mature faster than others, some of us will return home only to visit, others will return indefinitely, and their growth will be stagnated until they make that move to live on their own again. Only then will they be on their way to independence. We are not talking about someone who has to come into their parents' home to take care of them. That is a noble thing to do, and God promises us long life if we honor our parents and that's a promise that can't be broken. Isn't that something new already? How many times have I been disappointed by family and friends breaking promises? God will never break a promise, and all His promises were written in the Bible by men from different parts of the world in a span of four to six thousand years. Most of them did not know each other, yet they were all inspired without interruption. What a miraculous coordination only God can perform!

Now that you are on the other side, you are going to see unbelievable things happening in front of you. The more you learn about Him, the more He will reveal Himself to you, getting you to try to understand Him by looking at the facts and getting experience. While on this new journey, you will gain knowledge, but you have to make the move on your own. Mommy or Daddy can't do this for you. You have to move toward God on your own.

Finishing college does not give us all the knowledge that we need to make it in this world, but it helps point us in right direction. As we move into unfamiliar ground, we accumulate more information and know-how. There are so many paths in life. There are good paths, and there are bad paths. Some paths will lead us straight to jail, and some paths can give us a life worth living. If we have gotten on the path of trouble, in most cases, we put ourselves there. We make our own choices.

Now in many cases, because of a lack of knowledge, we put ourselves into some bad positions. This has to do with ignorance. Don't get offended. Ignorance just means lack of knowledge, or information. We know the old saying that knowledge is power, so as we begin this new life, we have to be around people who know about this new life. If we ask God, He will direct us to someone. There are many who will be able to help us on this journey when we are ready to embark on it. We have the power to make our own decisions, which can be good or bad, depending on how many facts we have. Anyone making a decision, or a choice without gathering facts is bound to fail. It's like driving a car down the street with a blindfold on. This is not to say that we still won't make mistakes, but this way, we can lessen them. Being young and naive will cause us to make mistakes, but we can't let this discourage us. We have to keep the faith and ask God to lead us down these uncharted paths and learn not to repeat the same mistakes. We must use that little voice inside of us and start to practice the gifts we have been given. Trust and believe that we were born with these talents. Every animal in the jungle has a unique quality that has been given to them for protection, from the porcupine to the various bugs in the grass. God gives everything a chance. We are made in His image, so we have what we need to protect us. We just have to learn how to tap into it.

Life can be hard as you go down its various pathways. At the beginning, the road may seem easy but then it starts to twist and turn, and things can get complicated. That's why God is needed at every twist in the road. Think God in all things—in every thought, every good deed, every word that comes out of our mouths—and He will direct our path. This is one of His promises, and God can't break His promises.

Now with that being said, there is a good and a bad at this junction. The bad is you don't know God's promises. When you were a child, do you remember your dad promising to take the whole family to a fun place that you loved more than anything? When he mentioned it, it made you so happy. You thought about it all day while you were in school, and when it was time to go to bed, you couldn't sleep. Your heart was pounding with excitement. You even had a dream you were there. Oh, how you couldn't wait! Who knows how many times you brought it up to your parents. And as promised, you and the whole family went, and you had the time of your lives, just as you had hoped. As you get to know God, you can magnify those feelings by a thousand times. But you have to learn about Him to receive His promises. See if your dad had not told you about the promise, how would you have known? There may have been times Dad, or Mom made promises they couldn't keep for whatever reason, but none of God's promises in the Word can ever be broken. This Word was started over six thousand years ago by our ancestors. They wrote the Word on animal skins, on walls in caves, and wood cut from tree trunks so that one day, we would find it and continue to pass it on from generation to generation.

Remember, knowledge is power. Never feel reluctant about picking up a book to read. As you continue to read books and sink your teeth into gaining knowledge, you will find that your brain will want more of this new information. As you continue to read the Word about God, you will open your horizons and expand your mind. The Bible is a work of art, and there is no other book like it in the history of mankind. It took writers over six thousand years to finish. There are copies in every language. Our ancestors knew how important it was to preserve these important documents to save us. They were inspired by the Holy Spirit to tell us about the Savior who would come and take away the sins of the world. Glory be to God for putting it in their minds and hearts to preserve it for us. There must be something in the Word they really wanted us to know.

Here we are, ready to see what's in store for us. It's been told to me that it is marvelous to live this new way and that it's like getting a new start in life, or getting a second chance at life. How do you get started? I never thought you would ask. You start out by getting to know Him for yourself, like you would when you first meet a person who you think is interesting. You start gathering all the information you can about that person. In this case, you will go to the Bible. There is so much information there that you have to take your time reading it. Reading this book is not like reading a book off the library shelf—it's difficult—but over time, if you stick with it and read a little each day, it will start to get into your spirit as it was designed to do. Trust this: Nothing good is easy to achieve, or else everyone would be doing it. You were chosen to be here at this point in your life. No matter how you got to this fork in the road, and some will never get here, so don't take it lightly. This is a very important time, and you will see what I mean later down the road.

You are on your way to an amazing relationship with God. The first thing that is going to enter your mind is *How can I have a relationship with someone who is not visible?* That's a healthy question. You walk by faith, and this is where it gets challenging. Once you are at the threshold, you are at the point of crossing over to the other side. It's a big step, but you will be on solid ground, and you will be well on your way. You see, you can't come to God unless you believe that He exists. Now that you want to start an intimate relationship with God, you start to walk with Him. You start to talk to Him. It may seem a little odd at first but that is how He talks back to you—through His Word. As you continue this process, you will notice changes in your life. The more you get to know Him, the more He will reveal Himself to you. Trust me, this will not be in vain. This relationship will enrich your spirit.

One of the things, that is so great about this affair is that you can trust God more than anyone on the planet because He will never let you down, or disappoint you. He will fulfill the promises that He has made in your life, and they will unfold right in front of your eyes. He knows the beginning and the end. It's always good to know someone who has that kind of power. No one but a divine spirit can know that, so forget about your horoscope, or palm readers. They are just telling you what your little ears want to hear. They play on emotions and false hope, and unfortunately, a lot of people rely on them, even though they don't know any more than the person who comes to them for their false readings.

To get to know God, you have to engage yourself in His Word and start to treat people like you would want to be treated. Now that can't be that hard. Remember that His yoke is easy. Try to put aside what you have heard and what you didn't get in the home when you were a child, what you weren't taught, and open your heart and mind to receive what already is inside you so that the faith can activate the spirit, or shall I say quicken the spirit. And the only way your faith can get stronger is by hearing the Word. Start with baby steps. There is no rush. And I know in a world like this with technology going in milliseconds that it is hard to slow down, but if you want this, you have to slow down to get the richness of the crop. First, the seed is planted in the earth, then God continues to nurture the crop with sunshine and rain until the kernel begins to protrude out of the earth. You see, it's time-consuming. This is a synopsis of how God works in you. His seed for you is His Word, and once it's in you, you become rooted in the Word, and all that goodness, joy, peace, happiness, and love comes out of you.

God never changes. He is the same yesterday, today, and forever. He will never let you down. He may not be there when you want Him, but He is always on time. He will never shame you on account of His Word. He will protect you if you stay in His grace. You are probably wondering how we know this. There were others before us who passed this information down to us. They were disciples like you will become one day, or maybe have already become. A disciple is a student in the following of Jesus Christ. As you become more knowledgeable about Jesus, you will want to start spreading His Word. The joy and happiness that you receive from learning His Word and the new love that you have for mankind will set your spirit on fire, and the only way to quench this fire is to run and tell everybody who will listen about it. You will surprise yourself. The beauty you have been seeking will come from the inside, and it will never fade away. You will also start to treat people differently. You will be concerned for their welfare and well-being. Your concerns will become more about human rights and equality for all than the movie stars and athletes that you used to idolize. I used to be more concerned about myself and mine, and now I'm about what part I can play to make this a better world. God will take care of the earth, and we as His disciples must focus on spreading His Word.

Reading the Word can be a little boring at first. You may have to look for a modern English version that leaves out the thous, thines, and thys, but as you continue reading, it becomes easier. If you start out only reading a chapter a day, that's okay. As you become consistent, you will start to understand that this is God talking to you. In return, you can talk to Him by praying to Him. As you become more knowledgeable, you will begin to see how He will give.

When we were little kids, we would look up at our dads like they were giants. We felt like we could go to our parents for anything because we trusted and depended on them to take care of us. Now that we are all grown up, we realize that our parents were depending on someone other than themselves. We couldn't see it then because they were so big and strong, but we see it now that they are becoming fragile. In some households, we used to see our parents pray. In others, we never heard the Word of God mentioned. Whether we heard the Word or not, our parents can't help us, like they used to when we were kids, and in some cases, we have to take care of our parents as they get older. This is how life goes. Once, our parents took care of us—they bathed and fed us—and now, it is our turn to return the favor.

God made us a promise because He knew this was going to happen: If we honor our parents, He promises we will have a long life. Even though God inspired man to write down His promises thousands of years ago, they are not in the past. They are His present promises to us. You may feel like you need that feeling of security and love that your parents once gave you, but what God has given you instead is full access to the strength, wisdom, courage, and love that He gave to your parents. It's been there the whole time. You just had to be ready to open your heart and mind to let the Savior in.

This book will refine you. God wants to remove hate, prejudice, envy, jealousy, anger, bullying, and all other impurities from our hearts. He is knocking at the door, and all we have to do is open it. Seek and you shall find. Ask and you shall receive. It's that simple, so simple that intelligent people will miss it. It will go right over their heads. It doesn't take a person who is philosophical, or highly educated to understand God. He made it so that everyone—simple, or educated, poor, or rich—can receive Him in their hearts if they choose. God made sure that if someone is deaf, blind, or mute, it won't be a barrier to following Him. No one on the planet can say that they didn't hear about God's Son, Jesus. This is one of the countless mysteries that God has for those who serve Him and are obedient to His Word.

You are on your way to gaining knowledge, wisdom, and understanding. You must realize by now that you are a special person. God made me special by giving me an assignment to do His will. My life was in shambles and in pieces that no one could put together but God. Like a potter who makes objects out of clay, God took the broken cup that was me and put the pieces back together. He took me back to clay and fixed my broken life. Then He made me special, not to sit on a shelf and be looked at but to carry out His will. Oh, how sweet it is to do the Lord's will. Nothing in the world compares to it. He will give you powers according to the Spirit working in you, powers to lift up people who feel like they are at the end of their rope. You have the power to give them hope to go on with their lives, power to give to the less privileged, power to lead by example.

At this stage of your new life, you may be asking yourself why you were chosen and not your sister or brother. You may be from a family that never spoke on the subject of God or had any kind of religious upbringing, so why you at this time in your life? It could be that it is up to you to lead by example, and when your family and friends see the way you are living, they may come and join you. Remember, this did not happen by chance. It was predestined that at this particular time in your life, you were going to be converted to help save your family from troubles that are lying ahead. There are so many mysteries about God that we don't fully understand. Consider discrimination, for example. All across this world, people are being discriminated against for being different, whether it's because of the color of their skin, or their beliefs. Intolerance starts in the home when we are little children, trusting our parents to instill beliefs in us that we can live by. Bear with me. I know this can be a really sticky subject. We carry our teaching deep in our souls, and a lot of us feel as though if we learn it from our parents, it has to be right because our parents would not tell us anything wrong, especially to hate someone for no apparent reason. I am not on this subject to say who is wrong, or who is right but rather to say that this type of thinking has been carried on for too long. God has given us the power to do away with it.

Case and point: If a doctor examines five cadavers of different ethnicity who had similar lifestyles and were a similar weight and age, he wouldn't be able to tell what color they were. So tell me, why do we as a people allow this type of ignorance to float through our society? Remember God has now given you the power to put a stop to things that poison our society. You must be a trendsetter and lead by example. Shut down those who speak ignorance to your ears and remind them that in God's family. It is not about hating one another.

It's about loving each other. Without blaming anyone, let's forgive them for they know not what they say, or do. Amen.

I need to tell you some things in advance so that when they happen, you will be prepared. Your family and friends are going to scrutinize you. They will probably place bets on how long you will last. You will become the talk of family gatherings. But I believe that you will find support within the family if you don't quit, or give in. Remember that in the long run, this is a positive change for you and your family. It is for your betterment. Be prepared to help the people entering your life in the near future, people whose lives you are going to change forever. You have been called upon at this very moment in your life to be a blessing for others. You are special.

You may think that you are not ready for this type of responsibility and decide to go back to the way your life was before you had this encounter. You can get back on the familiar path that you know well, or you can go on an adventure that will change you in ways you could never imagine. God is always going to give you the free will to make a choice. This is very important to Him because He wants a soldier who is willing to do His will and not someone with a bad attitude who feels like somebody is making him do this. Nah, we don't need that in the Body of Christ.

So if you are coming into this way of life, He doesn't want you to be lukewarm. He does not like that at all. You are finding your way, and just like a seed that has been planted in the earth, you have to be patient and let the seed grow. This encounter didn't happen by chance. This was predestined for you before the world began. Don't take this incident lightly. God has chosen you to do some work for Him. You did not choose Him. He chose you.

When you give yourself over to God, you will feel relief from the pressures of life because He will give you all the love and security that you could ever need. The bottomless pit that you were trying to fill with material objects will be filled to the top as soon as you accept Him into your life to fix all that is broken. You will have someone you can trust again, like when you were a child and trusted your parents. You will become part of a universal family of believers who help, encourage, love, and support one another. We feel real compassion for each other and treat each other, like brothers and sisters. We learn to love one another, like we love ourselves. A lot of us just want to be loved. Even people in power who condone violence and surround themselves with like-minded people want to be loved. These poor souls will never understand that God is in charge. He will come back to retrieve His people, and we will be judged by what we say and what we do.

Trials and tribulations will come and go in order to strengthen you on the inside and make your spirit grow. You will always have God by your side, and you will start to feel comfort in your trials knowing that they bring patience, endurance, and character. I pray that your love will abound more and more in the knowledge and depth of His insight.

FAITH

Faith is trust in the belief that whatever we are hoping for will come to fruition. Faith becomes stronger with practice. We have the power to bring things into existence through our faith. We just have to learn how to use it. Do you know that you have the power to heal the sick, just by touching them with your hands and that you can bless people with your words? You can do all these things by asking God for anything according to His will. And when you ask, do not waiver. Do not doubt that it will come to pass. It may happen immediately, or it may take some time, but it will come to pass.

You must be wondering how this works. Let's break it down. You come upon a man who is cold and hungry. You see his condition, and you say to him, "May God bless you." You honestly want God to bless him and that is good, but there is something else you must do before your faith will activate. You must act. You see that the man is hungry and cold, you have many coats, and so you give the man a coat and a warm meal. This shows that you truly meant well in blessing him. Faith is not going to serve you unless you do the work. For example, if you want a spouse, ask God for that and when you ask. Do it without doubting Him. Then start to prepare yourself by getting a job, a car, a house, or an apartment, anything that will support your desire for a spouse. In other words, start getting your life together as if it is going to happen, and it will come to pass.

Let me give you an even better example. Say you ask God for a job, but after asking, you stay in bed all day and never going out to look for a job. All the faith in the world is not going to help you land a job because you haven't done the footwork. If you go out to look for a job and have faith that you can get one, you will receive the blessing of God. God knows the plans He has for you, plans that will help you prosper and not harm you, plans that will give you hope and a future. We have to align ourselves with His will, and He promises that whatever we ask, it shall be given unto us. You have to trust and believe in Him who is able to do all things without fail.

Think about who you can trust in your life right now. You will probably name almost everybody you know, but as people, we are not infallible. We all come up short. We don't know what the next moment will bring, and when we turn to someone like ourselves, it's like the blind leading the blind. We all need help in our lives, so why not ask someone who knows all instead of asking someone who is guessing, like we are. If a person is rich, and you are needy, it does not mean that he, or she is better than you. If you have God, and they have money, who do you think is in a better position: the man who has the money, or the man who has God? Well, let's see, if the man who has money gets sick, do you think that if he prays to his money, he will get well? I'm going to go with praying to God to be healed. As a matter of fact, the man with the money will ask you to pray to your God for him. He can trust his money, and I'll trust my God any day of the week.

The more we start to learn about God, the more confident we become about ourselves. As we begin to trust God in all that we do, we begin to see the change in our lives. We lighten up, get loose, and start to enjoy the life that God wanted us to have from the beginning. We must understand that God will give us as much as we can handle without the chaos and anxiety that often comes with the things that we think might be best for us. Have you ever prayed for something and then had to pray to have it removed? I have, and I think I prayed harder for its removal than I did to receive it. So be careful what you pray for. It may haunt you.

You can take God with you everywhere because He is already there. You can call on Him day, or night because He never sleeps. The more belief you have in Him, the more power you will receive from Him to help your fellow brothers and sisters. Faith is like this: You take what you have, and you share it with someone who has less, and you do it from the kindness of your heart, not expecting anything in return because you know that God is going to make a way for you and your family. Your giving won't be in vain. You are on your way learning to put your faith in God. I have talked with countless Christians about their experiences with giving, and I can also testify that your labor will not be in vain. I've given to those in need—a coat, a pair of shoes, even a car—and in return, God blessed me with the car I always wanted, as surely as God lives. On your walk with God, I challenge you to try it.

When you do things like this, you activate God's power in you. See, in this stage of your faith, you have to trust in Him to provide for all your needs according to His riches. Well, I can guess what's on your mind. How rich is God? He owns everything on this planet. How do I know that? It's pretty simple: We come into this world naked, and we leave the same way. Not a single person since man has been on the earth has crossed over and taken all that they had with them. They might have had some things buried with them, but you know the rest of the story. We could have a debate about this. Even if a very rich person leaves his possessions with his children, the same formula is in effect. He is a God that's in us all, above us all and through us all.

Your faith is a valuable component in your walk with God. Remember, faith comes by hearing the Word and practicing it. The two have to go together. Just between you and me, most people will read a little of the Bible and that's it. They won't fulfill their potential. You must learn the Word, and you must practice it. Now this may sound like a lot of work. Well, let's see, when you go to the gym to work out, it's hard, but the harder you work, the better you look. So if you work out the Spirit, the better you will feel. The question: Do you want to look better, or do you want to feel better?

One of the many benefits of being on this path is that you can experience God's love while you are learning about Him. A lot of people don't want to follow the way because their parents did, and they think it's a boring life. Oh, how far from the truth that is! This is a happy life. There is so much to live for. There is so much to do. This life adds meaning to your life. You can get so busy that you wake ready to serve Him. See, it boils down to you serve God, or you serve the adversary because you cannot serve both. You love one, or you love the other.

I'll break it down a little further: You serve your flesh and its desires, or you serve the Spirit and the desire of God. We Christians do a lot of things: travel the world, go to parties, have friends, play games at the park. We just do it with a different mindset and in moderation. We do fall short in a lot of areas. I say this so you can know that none of us is perfect. We oftentimes think that you have to be perfect on this side. Not so. We are human, too, but as we walk with God, we become more confident in ourselves, and our choices are more in line with the Word of God. We don't just think and do, not caring who we might hurt, or what we might have done that we don't feel good about. We think with a conscience, and we think about the consequences of our actions. We invite the goodness that life has to offer and shy away from what can harm us. Everything about us is changing from the inside out. We are becoming more equipped to deal with life. Remember, just because we change our lives, don't mean that stuff doesn't happen to us.

Now that we have started to change our lives, it seems like we have more trials and tribulations. But we must hold onto God's unchanging hands. Whichever way life twists and turns, it is okay because God has our backs. All the challenges that we face are there to make us stronger on the inside, so count what you are going through as joy. Just make sure that you go through the mountain of trials and not around the mountain. It takes longer to go around trouble than it does to go through it and get it behind you, never to rise again.

I must say I thank God that He has designed it that we should become acquainted this way—that we could raise each other's awareness. If you have read this far in the book, you most likely are going through some trials. Trust me, these trials were always there. Think of how when your laptop slows down, and after you delete some of your unnecessary files, it speeds back up. This is how your trials are going to be eliminated from your life. Instead of slowing you down, you come to a state where integrity leads the way, and your conscience becomes your monitor. If you grow in the way, you will be tested by your faith. God will allow things to happen in your life to see how you react to them. In some cases, people run back to their old way of life and don't deal with the problem, or they buy things to get their minds off the problem, but this is when you stand up and allow God to get you through it. You are already victorious. You just have to go through the process. We are always victorious when we stick by God. He knows all. We don't. When you are at the threshold and fearful of the unknown, stick with it and don't go back. You are in position. Now you can begin to walk in blind faith. This is the best there is—to walk in blind faith, trusting in God for your every move, trusting Him when you can't see what's around the next corner.

We must remember that we are babies in Christ, and we are going to make mistakes. We are, in many cases, going to fail the test, but as long as we stay on the course that's been designed for us, all will be well. God will never give you more than you can bear. At the beginning, He will give you little tests. As your faith grows, He will give you bigger tests. Don't take this personally. He does this to all of us who come into the way. You will know the outcome of your test once you go through it. And the tests, or trials you go through make you stronger and give you the ability to help the next person who may be struggling through a painful trial. When you start to complete these trials, you will see the reward on the other side. You will be able to tell someone about your testimony.

I want you to know that you didn't get to this place on your own. It was divine order from God. He has something for you to do. It could be that you are going to save a thousand souls from going to hell by your words, or behavior, or it could be that you save just one soul. That's just as valuable to God because the one soul you save might be yours. We don't try to figure God out because His thoughts are much greater than we could ever conceive.

God will be with you in the midst of your trials. He promises to never leave us, so we are never alone. We may feel that we are sometimes, but it's not so. God will not forsake you. This is His promise, and He does not lie. Men and women may deceive you, but God's promises you can stand on. What you put into this new life is what you will get out of it—zero equals zero. You have to deposit something into your bank account to withdraw something. That's just the way it works. The more you work toward this new way, the more you will be rewarded. That's God's promise. You have to trust Him in order to get past these little bumps in the road. If this was easy, everyone would be doing it. But this is not for everyone.

To get to where you are going, you have to go through some trials, and some are going to be very difficult and challenging. But if at this point in your journey you knew the rewards, you would count your trials as joy and welcome the hardships that accompany them. Carry on with your calling, and when you reach your potential, you will teach others to follow you into His marvelous light. We have to have some cloudy days in order to appreciate the sunny days. Lift up your bowed heads and walk upright. You are being watched by God and His angels. Let's praise Him for what He is doing in our lives and in our family's lives. Thank Him because He is worthy of being praised. He is preparing for you to do great and mighty work.

Stadium versus Church

People attend collegiate and professional sporting events by the thousands. They fill the stadiums to full capacity on any given day, or night and spend hundreds of dollars a game for a little less than two hours of entertainment. And if we really thought about it, we would probably ask ourselves why. I'm not saying that people should not have a good time and enjoy themselves, but what I'm saying is why do we lift athletes so high on a pedestal? Why do we pay so much to see some men play sports? We pour our hearts out for these athletes, and once the game is over, that's it. What good came out of the event? You walk away with a loss. In each sport, there are only so many players and so many teams and yet a big percentage of our children want to play on one of these teams. Do you know the chances of your child making it to the professional level? It's like hitting the lottery. And yet we encourage and work these children to the bone to be something they might not even want to be.

So we must look a little deeper to find out who's at fault: the child, or the parents. Sports are supposed to be fun, not a job for a young kid who thinks that he has to do this so he can make his parents happy. People have to ask themselves when they are at the games and acting out with other parents, fighting each other while the kids are supposed to be having fun, did you even ask your child if this is what they wanted to do? Or have you swayed them into thinking that they don't have a choice, telling them this is what they are going to do? Is this what we wanted for ourselves but could not achieve, so we put the pressure on them? I only can imagine the number of children who are only participating in sports to please their grown parents. The adults have taken the fun out of the game. I'm not saying that all kids feel this way, but maybe your child wants to be a doctor, lawyer, preacher, scientist, or an engineer.

I would like to set up this scenario. Let's say on a given day it is announced that Michael Jordan and LeBron James are going to be at a certain location at one in the afternoon signing autographs and giving away their brand-name shoes, and at the same time, one mile away, a church is going to be having a service for people to get to know Jesus. Which event do you think the crowd will be attending? We can go back and forth on this, but I'm a realist. If you really look at what's happening in our world today, you know people would choose to see the basketball players.

We need to look at where our society is headed and consider slowing down the pace. There are things showing up on television and on our cellular phones that used to be unthinkable. We used to give our kids cell phones in case of an emergency, but now babies are getting phones for their fifth birthdays and in some cases, sooner. Where does it stop? Where do we draw a line on this? We see someone else do it, and we join in whether it's right, or wrong. We have to stop following the crowd. Just because it seems like everyone is going a certain way does not mean that they are right.

This brings me to a point in the Bible that states, "Wide is the path to destruction and narrow is the path to life." The narrow path is hard to find. We worship people who are in the limelight, but we really don't know who they are. We want to be like them, or look like them, not realizing they are just like us. It's okay to admire their talents but not to want to be them. It's hard for young children to understand that these people make mistakes just like we do, so we must tell them that the person they want to emulate is just the same as they are. They are not as good as we make them out to be. They are human just like us.

Stadiums came into existence thousands of years ago when Rome was running the world. The emperors, who made the people worship them as gods, wanted to gain popularity among the people, so they had men fight to the death in stadiums as a form of entertainment. The fighters were called gladiators. The emperor would get common men and condemned criminals to battle the trained gladiators, and thousands of people would come out to enjoy the spectacle. This type of entertainment still goes on to this day. The lesson here is it's not always good to follow the crowd. Don't take part in something because everyone else is taking part in it. You must consider whether it's something that is good for you as an individual. You have to stand on a solid foundation and look at what is really going on. People are creating all kinds of havoc in our society today, and we just go along to get along and that's not the answer.

Case and point, iPhone and other cellular phone manufacturers come out with a new version on an average of every six months or so, give or take a month or two. They label their phones with the next highest number, iPhone 5, iPhone 6, and we buy the new phone just because of the number, not the phone itself. As I said earlier, I'm a realist. You tell me what's the difference between an iPhone 8 and a 9, or for that matter what's the difference between a ten and eleven? You tell me how far these companies are going to take it. Are we going to see a number twenty? I use this particular number because I hope to finish the book before they get to twenty. I must hurry. They are going at a very fast pace. If your friend has a number ten phone, and you have a number seven, it does not mean that your friend has a better phone. As a mass stadium of people, we all try to keep up with the Joneses, and we do this in almost every area of our lives.

I use the cellular phone example because everyone has one, from the rich to the poor, from the senior citizen to the toddler. At eighteen months old, my grandbaby knew how to do things on the phone that I did not know how to do. When I asked her how she did that, how she got into my phone's pass code, she started speaking baby language. You know where that went. We have to know where to draw the line. Now we have to ask ourselves, "What more can they put in that little device to get us to keep buying the next number?"

I can tell you now that the masses at the stadium will not be reading this book, although I pray that they will because God wants everyone on the planet to get to know Him. God wants all the people who came on the planet before us and those who are here with us and those who will come after us to know Him. He wants to give each of us the chance to get this. We all will be given the opportunity. You won't be able to say I was blind, or I was deaf, or I was lame. Are you too busy to let Him into your life? Are you so busy trying to keep up with the masses, the stadiums of people who will hear of Him but who won't accept Him? He does not pressure anyone to come to Him. In fact, He would rather you come to Him joyfully and not grudgingly. We are not doing Him a favor by coming to Him. He does not need us. We need Him. We are here to help each other, but we have strayed from this important principle. The good thing is it's never too late to get back on the path. We just have to redirect our energies. There is nothing that we can't do together. There is power in numbers, and together we stand, or divided we will fall. What a different place this would be if everyone, rich and poor, would roll up their sleeves and start working together. I guess that is asking for a lot, especially when there are individuals who hoard food from starving people. It seems impossible to believe, but it's true. Don't forget about the idol whom you so much want to be like, who has a house with twenty bathrooms, spending hundreds of dollars to get to see them for less than a few hours. I'm just saying how many bathrooms can a single person use in a day? One. That's right, only one. I'm just being a realist. I don't expect a lot of people to listen to this, or for things to change. I'm just raising your awareness.

People can be very cruel, and we take it just to get along. The question: How high is your tolerance level? Some people can run behind the masses all their lives. They are just made that way, but you are not made like that. You are meant to share the many virtues that you have—compassion, love, joy, kindness. You just have to learn how to tap into them. I'm not saying others don't have them. They just choose not to use them. Some of us have different gods, and if you are not with their gods, you have no place with them. Our God is all loving, thoughtful, caring, and has all power in heaven and on earth. It does not matter who their god is. There is only one living God, and He made us. He never sleeps, or slumbers. He is always watching and protecting us. He will never let us down. He may not give us what we want, but He will always give us what we need. He knows us because He made us, and He breathes His Spirit in all of us. He gave us a free will to serve Him or to do as we want. Remember the hardships that you are going to go through. That's how He makes you worthy to be one of His. He chastens those He loves, like you do with your children. You would not chasten someone else's child, would you? Of course not. Nothing makes a parent prouder than seeing their children doing well and staying out of trouble. The children who turn out the best are the ones who listen to what their parents tell them. Our parents will never lead us into harm's way, at least not intentionally. Why children and young adults don't listen to their parents is a mystery of deep waters.

Let's get off the subject of the masses and talk about the places we go to worship. We call these places churches, and others call them temples, or mosques. We have many churches in our country. Some cities have a church on every block. Some churches have only a few members and some have thousands. Only a small percentage of our population actually attend church services. There is an infamous saying about church: "Dollar bills go to church, and one-hundred-dollar bills go to the casino."

I can safely say that the stadiums are attended by the masses, and the church are attended by the few. But how can this be when there are hundreds, even thousands of churches in a city and only one casino? On any given day, a casino brings in one to five million dollars, whereas churches are struggling to keep their doors open. This is a mystery of deep waters. Something is wrong here. We as a people need to look into this. We have every kind of commercial on the airwaves telling us how to spend our money. We have big commercials advertising candy for Halloween, shopping on Black Friday, and toys for Christmas. Christmas is supposed to be about Jesus's birthday. Why are we exchanging gifts with each other? It's not our birthday. These holidays are merchants' biggest moneymakers, and they seem to be adding more, like Cyber Monday. Where do we draw the line? Have you seen the lines outside stores? People wait in line for days to get a new phone, or game so they can be the first to get it. What is the meaning of this? It's a mystery of deep waters.

Grown men and women earn millions of dollars a year to play sports, yet first responders, who risk their lives every day, earn between twenty-five thousand dollars and fifty thousand dollars a year. They are not playing a game. They put their lives second to the people they save. Yes, this, too, is a mystery of deep waters. It is obvious that our society is missing the mark. We have lost our perspective.

How can we change this phenomenon? We can't change the way this is going. It has been going on for too many generations. It will take many generations more to get back on track. Some of us are on automatic pilot. We don't take the time to think about what we are doing and why we are doing it. We, the few, and our generations down the line have to step up to the batting box and start swinging for a change. We can start by getting to know about God, accepting Him as our Lord and Savior, and having our children get to know and accept Him too. The only way this can be fixed is by going to the Source. We are on the wide path to destruction. In the words of a dear auntie of mine who is in the church, "Let those who have eyes to see, see."

Those of us who are in the church must go outside the church's secured walls and get more involved in the community. God is gracious. He loves us all the same, even those who don't believe in Him. We have forgotten what Jesus said: Spread the Word to Jerusalem, Judea, Samaria and to all corners of the world. We pray and ask God to do things for people, yet we do nothing when He calls upon us to act. Church folks, we have the power. We let fear, or a lack of faith stop us from using the power that God has given us. Remember the lesson of the race between the coney and the river cutter: The coney was so far ahead that he decided to get some sleep. When he awoke, the river cutter was at the finish line. It is time for the church to wake up. Our work is not finished. We have become too laid-back. We are God's servants. Do we want the master to catch us sleeping?

In the parable of the talents, the master was going away for a time, and he left one servant ten talents, another servant five talents, and another one talent. When the master returned, he asked his servants to come forward to find out what they had been doing in his absence. The one with ten talents doubled his talents, the one with five talents also doubled his, but the servant with one talent hid his talent. The master was very angry at the one who hid his talent. To the church: We are hiding the God-given talents that were freely given to us. When we were hot in the Lord, we got the power. We just don't have the faith to use it.

I understand that Moses was afraid to go and fight for God at first. Moses had all kinds of excuses, and God had an answer for his weak responses. Saints, are you making weak and feeble excuses to the God who saved you so that you can help save others? Remember, we are soldiers in battle formation, fighting the unseen battle, which is not our battle but His. We have to show up and go where God positions us. All we have to do is be ready, and God will fight the battle for us. Is that not what He said? He gave us a manual to guide us, but we have to read it. To know what we have been given by the Father, ask God to give you His Holy Spirit to lead and guide you, and let us train to become warriors for Christ. For Christ said, "Deny yourself, pick up your cross, and follow me." We must travel outside the walls of the church, outside our comfort zone, and go fishing for men and bring them inside the church so that they can have what we have in Christ. Amen.

Saints, if every church was to practice going into the community regularly, showing its presence, what do you think would happen? It's a no-brainer. Jesus spoke so much about love in His short time with us, but do we practice love? He said that those outside the church will know us by the love we show one another. Preachers, you must preach what the Lord said, not what you think the congregation wants to hear. A lot of Christians think that once they are saved, they won't have pain and suffering in their lives. The preachers are saying if you get saved, you will have big houses and lots of money coming from places unknown. All this stuff does not satisfy your soul. We have our instructions and that's what should be preached to the saints. We need disciples, not members. We need quality, not quantity. We can't stop at being taught about the Word. We have to go out and practice what we have been taught. That is what strengthens our faith. The church has to get back to its original place in society so that the masses can follow us.

When a newcomer joins the church, we must protect them and teach them about the way in the same way that we were taught. This is very important. We must teach the way the Bible instructs us without adding to it, or taking away from it. Different groups are coming out with all kinds of movements to validate their experiences. We in the church have lots of valid reasons to build a strong movement for God to save souls. We really need to get God's church back in order. Have we lost focus on what we were saved to do? The Father left explicit details on how we were to carry out His great mission. But it is not being preached that we should step outside the gate of the church and go after the lost souls. Once we are found, we are spending more time getting members than teaching disciples. There is no way on God's earth that the church should be divided. I believe that these preachers are intimidated by one another, by who has the most members and who has the biggest church. Remember, preacher man, it's not about you. It's about Him. You have been chosen to carry out God's plans. You know what you were called to do. You know that this is not His kingdom. Don't you help people believe that the rewards are here? God's rewards for those who earn them are put away in heaven so that no man can steal them. And His biggest reward is for those who show blessings to the needy. He says, "What you have done for the least of them, so you have done for me."

A preacher is called by God to shepherd the people. Tell me how can one man shepherd ten thousand members? I'm pretty sure God called enough preachers to watch over His people until His return. There should be cooperation among the preachers to aid and assist one another, but instead, all these churches are doing their own thing. It wasn't meant to come to this. You pastors were called and ordained by God. I believe that God is going to stir your spirit up to make the changes we need to continue God's work as He gave it to us.

To all the leaders of the churches, look inside yourselves to find out what God wants you to do. From this point on, forget about the past, and let's get back on the path that the Father has prepared for us to go down. In the congregation, let's start to show one another more love. Let's not be jealous of one another. We have to continue to grow in this process. We have to work on ourselves to be more like Jesus. This advice is for all of us. We all fall short. When we come upon a situation, we should think, *What would Jesus do in this situation.* He gave us a royal command and a golden rule that we should follow to make the world a better place to live. It's a simple set of rules: Love God with all your heart, mind, soul, and strength; and love your neighbor as you love yourself. And the golden rule is to treat people as you want to be treated. If we all practiced this, the world would be a nicer place to live in. There would not be so many wars. There would not be as much hate. We can right our course by being obedient to the Word. The most important work for the church is to spread the Word and save souls. We must not lose the focus. As a member of God's house, you have been called upon. Have you been obedient to His Word, or have you been overcome with fear? It's all right. I feel you. It's hard to step out of your comfort zone when God calls you up. I know firsthand because He is using a broken cup, like me. I was shattered, like a cup that fell on to a concrete pavement and broke into many pieces. If it was anybody but God, I would have been tossed into the waste bin. But God put me back together and is using me for a special task. I don't want to do it. I can really understand why Moses made all those excuses. It makes me laugh just thinking about what God has called on me to do. When He calls on you, it's like. You either accept, or deny Him. Don't let such an amazing opportunity pass you by. Remember He doesn't call everyone for these special assignments. If you don't rise to the occasion, He will move on to someone who is worthy of the task.

Now you know why not everyone is a real Christian. Those of us who have been called are His servants. You see, in this world, many of us look at who has the highest position in the church and at work and aim to please them. In God's kingdom, He looks at the servants who will go and do His will, which is spreading His Word and saving souls. If we say we love Him who we have never seen but do not love our brother who we see every day, that's a mystery of deep waters. Let us rekindle our fire, so we can start our movement with love leading us on the way.

I'm still talking to church folks here. With churches on almost every corner, how come are we not united? The church needs to be united as one. There is but one God, one faith, one baptism, so why do we have different denominations? God didn't do that. Man has done this to God's works. We are the people who God left in charge until His return. He entrusted us with His Word. There should not be a homeless person in the world, or a person who is lacking food. In America, we throw away enough food to feed the whole continent of Africa. So what is happening in the church and where it is heading is a mystery of deep water.

Once we get saved, we, being the church folk, do a good job of helping those who make it to church become wholesome, but what about those who never get inside the walls of the church? Do we just forget about them, or do we say to them, "It's up to you to come to church, and once you come in, we will help you"? Do we disregard those who can't make it? By all means no. This is not how it is done. God knew we would do it this way. He knew once we got our hides saved, we would stay in the pen. This is only because we really don't know the power that God has given us. Do you remember when we first got saved? We were on fire. We were telling everyone that we ran into that we were saved, but as time went on, we stopped growing in Christ. We became lukewarm. What happened to our audacity? Why did fear creep into our Christian lives? The work is not over. It has just begun. Now is the time for us to step outside the doors of the church and go to the highways and byways and save some souls with the power that is invested in us. God did not transform us so we could hoard it. No, we must go outside and help those who are in the same place we used to be because we are all ex-something—ex-liars, ex-thieves. I speak from the heart. A preacher cannot speak these kinds of words because he will lose a lot of his congregation. If Jesus suffered, why do you think you won't have to suffer? Did you not hear God say He will chasten those He loves? Don't you know how the prophets suffered? Or how the early church was persecuted in the name of Jesus? His followers were arrested and tortured so they would renounce His name. If they would not renounce His name and not disclaim Him, they were put to sleep. Would you go through all that torture for Jesus? Let's be honest. God knows your heart, so the answer that you give is between you and the Son. He knows our thoughts and our deepest secrets. Confession is good for the soul.

Now we the church are ready for you newcomers in Christ. We are waiting for you with open arms. We are going to love you, like you are our biological children. We are going to do all we can to make you comfortable in this new way just as we were treated, or better, for we know how much God loves us. We are going to display the same love that God has poured out on us, not an ounce less. We know the measure we give will be given back to us. It's time for those of us who have been in the church for years to step up to the plate and practice what the Holy Spirit has been teaching us—step out on some blind faith. You know what I'm talking about—not knowing but moving on the Word of God.

As a newcomer to the church, you are saved by confessing to Jesus as your Lord and Savior and believing in your heart that He died for your sins. He is the first of the resurrected to be alive, and He is seated on the right side of God. This is a lot to take in at first, so take small steps and connect with a Bible-teaching church so you can be protected as you grow. What you put into it is what you will get out of it. There are promises in the Word that are yours for the asking of Him. These blessings have two parts: One part is for you to carry out, and the other part is for God to bring to pass. Remember when your parents told you if you were good, you would get what you asked for? Well, it works the same way with God. If you do your part, the Father will reward you. Rewards don't always come in the form of money. There are better rewards than money that come in the form good health, good children, a loving family, peace, joy, or happiness.

Remember we are saved to help others be saved. We are a great big family, and we should always treat each other as such. You see, God is love, and He pours His love out to His children, and we give our love to each other. That's how we love one another. It is said in the Word that true religion is helping the widow and the orphan and be on the path of righteousness, so the church has to always have open arms when one of these souls comes for refuge.

We are going to get back on track, and God is going to do amazing things with the church. We are going to have to step up and do what God has commanded us to do. God is watching those of us who were put here to carry out what His disciples started over two millennia ago. We will have to account for our deeds. We should be saving souls at a much faster pace. We expect God's best, so we must give our best. That's only fair.

As a newcomer to the church of the Body of Christ, we are going to pray that you get the strength to endure the trials that are in front of you. Don't think you are being picked on. We all have to go through the fire. It strengthens us and gets us ready for God's purpose and the plans He has for us to carry out. A reverend who I love dearly says, "We are not going to rust out. We are going to wear out," meaning get prepared to be a disciple and go out and spread the word of salvation to everyone. Again, I must remind you that you didn't just fall into this. This was supposed to happen. You have the power to move along this path. The Father will put a lamp under your feet and a light in your path. He will direct your path, so acknowledge Him in all that you do.

Are you going to continue on this new path, or go back to what you were doing? The choice is yours. God would never force you to make a decision. We must remember that He does not need us. We need Him. When it comes to making up our minds to come to Him, He will never let us down, or leave us, or forsake us. He says He will be with us until the end of the world and that, my brothers and sisters, is one of the many promises He has made and has never been broken. As you take these small steps on your new journey, hold onto his unchanging hands.

I think it is important to explain a little more about these different paths of life that we are walking down but can't yet see. When you look up in the sky and see an airplane, that plane is on a particular coarse, but you can't see it. In fact, the pilot who is flying the plane cannot see the path either. The air traffic controller in the control tower at the airport is controlling what direction the plane is going in, and he lets the pilot know what's ahead of him and whether he should take the plane up a few thousand feet, or down a few thousand feet. The air traffic controller sees everything that's in the path of the plane. If it were not for him, the pilot could not get from point A to point B. The pilot has to put his trust in the air traffic controller, and the people on the flight have to put their trust in both of them. We don't know who they are, whether they are on drugs, or alcohol, or mentally challenged, or if on this particular day, they may want to end it all and selfishly take others with them. There are so many variables at play here, but mercifully, it seems to work. We can thank God for that.

God is the controller of all our lives. He knows the beginning of all our lives, and He knows the end. He is everywhere at the same time. He does not sleep, or slumber. He is always watching us. Who would not want a God with all these powers? It's a mystery of deep waters. If we stay in the dark, we can never know the awesome God that we serve. He is the Alpha and Omega. There is nothing that happens on this earth that He doesn't know about. He even knows when a bird falls out of a tree to its death before it has hit the earth. He knows the number of hairs on your head by each strand. He knows what you are thinking before you do. All we have to do is believe and trust Him, and we will be well on our way. Just as we exercise our bodies, we have to exercise our spirit and faith. We can either continue to feed the body and be enslaved by the adversary, or we can feed the spirit and be enslaved by God. We cannot serve both.

When we feed the body, we feed it with food and water, both of which are necessary to continue to live. But the body yearns for much more. It yearns for sex. Not a little, it wants multiple partners. The body feeds on excessive eating, excessive alcohol and drugs, and excessive spending. It wants excess in all areas in order to continue to fill its bottomless pit. And still, that's not enough. It also feeds on hate in every area: color, creed, religion. I can go on and on, but you get the picture. The body is never satisfied, and you become a slave to this yoke around your neck.

So how do we feed the spirit? We feed it through God's Word. It gives us sound instructions and corrections. It teaches us to ignore the wants of the body. And as we continue to say no to the body, we become stronger in the spirit. When we feed the spirit and starve the body of all its wants and needs, the spirit feeds us with love, joy, and happiness. The more you deny the flesh, the more your spirit grows. Now I don't mean that you should stop eating and starve yourself, but eat in moderation, do outside things in moderation. We have to try and do what we can and when we can't. We must ask God for guidance. He will bring people into our lives who can help us overcome our weaknesses. In this way, we give ourselves to the Lord. There is nothing that we can ask of Him that He won't grant.

When you are really saved, that's when the real work begins. I know it's been said before that this is not the time to be lazy. You have to help out in saving souls. Please, I beg you, don't start trying to impress one another. You have to roll up your sleeves and get to work. He has chosen you to come from darkness into the light. Would you take a light and cover it with a blanket? No. You would put it on a stand so that everyone in the room could see. That's what you have to do with the light that the Father has given you. Let your light shine so that everyone can see and want what you have. Make sure that you read the Word for yourself so that you can share your Christian experience with others. In all the relationships I know of, you try to get to know everything about the one you love, and to get to know God, you must get to know His Word. You must be able speak from your own experience when people ask you what you do and how you do it. If you don't read your Bible, all you can say to them is what you have heard someone else say about their experiences with the Father and His Son and that is not right. You know that. If you don't read, how are you going to know all the power He has given you? You say you believe. You have the power of life and death in the tongue. He told us that, but if you don't read, how are you going to know what He has promised?

As I mentioned earlier, the Bible is a book written by men and women who were inspired by the Holy Spirit. They were chosen and deemed worthy of the calling to write the Bible and go from city to city to spread the Gospel, which means Good News. They sacrificed their lives to get His Word to our ears. Remember faith comes to us by hearing. They were persecuted and put in jail, and they were executed as they tried to get the Word out to the people who were chosen to continue to run with it. They wrote the Word on walls in caves. They wrote the Word on scrolls and even on clay tablets so that we could have it some two thousand years later. Did they think that what they wrote down would be read thousands of years later? Of course not, but they had the hope in the power that was vested in them. God's promise to Abraham over six thousand years ago was brought to pass and passed down in the pages of the Word to the present time. The promise He gave Abraham are the same promises we have today because we are the descendants of Abraham. By faith and belief in the Father, we are credited with righteousness. The Bible is not like any other book. No other book even comes close to it, and no other book has had more copies published, yet only a small percentage of people have read it. Now that's a mystery of deep waters.

I'm trying to finish this chapter, but I keep being fed, so I must feed you. It would be an injustice to my soul to not to give it to you as I am getting it. I love the church just that much. I want to put this as gently as I can because this next problem is a real big disappointment in the church. The Bible is a book of instruction and correction on how to live a righteous life. But we don't want to be corrected and instructed on how we should live our lives. When the preacher is preaching the Word, we might think, *My sister, or my brother needs to hear this message.* But really, the message is for us. The Word is a double-edged blade. It cuts both ways. We must stop letting our denial protect us. We have to look inside ourselves in order to change.

The Word is a seed that has to get inside of us in order to grow. If we don't read the Word, we will be the same person we were when we were in the dark. Yes, we have people in the church who are saved but have not changed. They are going to church but keeping up chaos they were doing before they were saved. This is why it is so hard to get people to venture outside the church walls to save others. We have so much to do, yet we think when we get saved that's it. We know better than this. We know that God does not work that way. He wants all of us to be saved. He made hell for Satan and his demons, not for us. If you want to begin to change, you have to start to read the Word. A lady asked me what she should do when she doesn't understand the Bible. I had a quick answer for her: Ask the Holy Spirit because He is the teacher.

The Bible tells us that when Jesus was getting ready to ascend to the right hand of the Father, Jesus told his disciples to go back to Jerusalem to wait for the gift that He was going to send. He was speaking about the Holy Spirit, which had not yet been given. When He sent the gift of the Holy Spirit, the Apostles were able to remember and understand everything that Jesus had taught them. So the Holy Spirit is our teacher. Call on Him when you start to read the Word, and it will be like when a farmer plants a seed in the earth, and God does a number on the seed. That is how the Word works. Once God plants the Word in you from your reading, He will renew your mind and change your heart. When someone says that you look different and act different, you can say you are a servant of the living God and tell them what the good Lord has done for you. Yell it to the mountains. Let them know that when you first get saved, the little trials might seem like mountains but that is nothing compared to what the Father has prepared for you. Eyes have not seen, ears have not heard, and the heart cannot conceive of the amazing things He has waiting for us. They are there just waiting for us to finish the race. See, the race is not for the swift and the strong. It is for those who endure. So continue to run down this path, and you will endure the trials on the highway to heaven.

Belief

We can't begin to know how many souls have entered and left this world since God made man, but there is an estimated six to seven billion people on the planet at the present time. We are spread all over this planet. We are different colors, we speak different languages, we have different beliefs, we wear different clothing, and even eat different foods. It is no secret that our first teachers are our parents, God bless their souls, and what we learned from them we take with us when we become adults. We never questioned what we were taught by our parents because we trusted them to have our best interests at heart. We absorbed the good and the bad. Our parents' teachings were repeated over and over until they became a part of us. It's safe to say that a lot of us pass our home training on to our children. Unfortunately, some things our parents taught us were not all that good. Some things they taught us were pretty bad, like those people are different, they're a different color, or they dress differently, so don't mix with them, or those people are bad, they don't go to the same kind of church as we do. It's not our parents' fault. Their parents taught them the same things they taught you. This hate and fear may go back hundreds, or even thousands of years.

So as we go along in a life of hating, we start to split hairs on who to hate and who not to hate. We start hating without a cause, and this hate goes deep into our souls. We may have been taught that people who are different from us are not human, or that they are animals, and we believed this to be true because we got it from those we trusted with our dear lives. We were too young to filter this teaching out, so we went along with this evil thinking, and some of us carry it to this day. Many people have died believing this hatred and taking it to their graves. Millions of people have been murdered on this principle. Even today, people kill others because of their color, or religion. We have wars going on right now because of religion and God. Can you believe that children are being taught to kill, and they don't question it? They hate without a cause. They believe so hard that they are doing God's will. They think that if a person is not the same religion that they have the right to eliminate them. It seems hard to believe that all it takes for an innocent and precious child to become a monster of hatred is to teach him or her to hate without a cause.

Hate has flipped the world upside down. We are all stewing in a pot of hate toward one another. Parents, give our children a break. Cut this cancer out of your family line. All hate has caused is wars and more wars. The reward we get for hate is death and destruction. We know from reading the Word who has that kind of behavior. It's the adversary. He comes to steal, kill, and destroy. It's so easy in this great country to recruit people into hate groups because they have been taught to hate at home without questioning it.

What we learn as children has a big influence on the way we conduct ourselves as adults. If we don't watch out, hate will be passed down through our families, like diabetes, cancer, and other inherited diseases. The difference is that diseases are passed down through our genes, and hate is passed down through stupidity and ignorance. These teachings and behaviors are like leeches. They suck out all the good that's in us.

You can't teach love and hate in the same household. One is going to outweigh the other. How can a person who loves teach their children to hate? It does not work that way. In most of these households, they didn't teach about God because they were too busy teaching about hate. You see, God is love, and just because you didn't learn about Him does not mean He does not exist. At the very least, you were called on to stop the hate in your family. God has called you to teach your children to love and to show love. It is time for you to turn this thing around. There is not enough time to blame your parents, so use your energy to make the necessary changes. Once you accept God who is all love, you will achieve a different perspective. That hate that you held so deep in your soul will start to diminish, and love in God will teach you to teach your children differently.

With God, there is peace, and we can use a lot of that. We have to believe that God exists. If that is too hard at this stage of your life, take a step toward Him, and He will take a step toward you. You will see that the Lord is good. If you believed all the hate, why not try believing in love? Nobody said this was going to be easy. Remember you are the trendsetter of your family. You are going to make changes for your family so that when your innocent children grow up, they will represent you with the life you taught them to lead. If you believe in Him, all things are possible—things like turning your family around and introducing them to something that they never had in their lives. You cannot leave your parents out of this new way of life. You will be blessed, and your family will be blessed also.

I know what you are thinking. *I want you to believe in something you can't see.* Well, just because you can't see it doesn't mean it doesn't exist. You feel the frigid wind blow when you walk to your car on a cold winter day, but you don't see it. When you look out your living room window in the fall, and you see the leaves blown around on the ground and carried into the air like a funnel, you see the activity of the wind. You see and feel the invisible wind that comes from God. The wind does not come from man. Let's not get it twisted. The meteorologists get paid to give us the weather report, and they are wrong 70 percent of the time. It is the only job in the world that pays someone to be wrong. They have computers and all kinds of gadgets. They have radars going hundreds of miles in each direction, and yet they still have a very low rate of being right. At the end of the day, even with all their high-tech equipment, they still don't get it right. This is because only God knows, which way He is taking the wind.

God sends the wind across oceans, continents, states, counties, and cities to reach your backyard, and no man, or woman can say where it comes from, or where it is heading. You may tell yourself that you can't see Him, but if you take the time to know Him, you will feel Him and see Him in your daily life. You must believe that He exists, and once you slow down to learn about Him, you will hear that little voice you always heard start to get louder. As you start to read about God in the Bible and hear the Word, your belief will become stronger and stronger. Remember this is not a race. It's for those who endure. You must develop patience and that takes practice. I know we live in a world where the internet can't go fast enough. It moves in seconds and that's what we have become accustomed to, but to get this, you are going to have to slow your roll.

Where do you start if you were never taught about God? You start at the beginning. You start as a little kid. You have to be like a young child wanting to get information. You have to chew and digest the Word and then live it so it can transform you into what God wants you to be. He has something for all of us to do. We have to quiet ourselves and listen for His voice, which could come from a brother, or sister in Christ, or from a vision, or a dream. His message will come when you are supposed to receive it.

God gave you a compass to help you navigate the paths that you can't see with your vision. It leads you down the road of righteousness. It's that little voice that you have been hearing all your life that has never been wrong. How many times have you thought that you should have listened to your first thought instead of listening to a friend, or a family member? I'm not saying that everyone who knows God is right. What I'm saying is you have to get wise counsel.

Let's consider this example: If you are having marriage problems, you wouldn't go to a person who is not married for advice. A blind person can't be taught by someone who is also blind. They have to be taught by someone who can see the light. We see the light. Come ye all that are in darkness into His marvelous light so that you don't stumble along the path that has been set out for you. If you don't know the way, you have to pray and ask God to send one of His servants to help you along the way until you can see the light. Then you return the favor by helping another person who is in the dark. Our mission is to help one human being at a time. Once you start to believe, you become, as I am, a servant of Christ. You wouldn't want to hide the light, would you? No. You want to walk in a room and let your light shine so you can start using your God-given powers and start saving souls.

You did not just stumble upon this. It was destined before you were in your mother's womb that you would be introduced to God at this time and not a second before, or a second later. A man plans his life, but God orders his steps. Trust me, it is better for Him to order your steps than for you to plan something when you don't even know what the next moment will bring into your life! The God we serve is omniscient, omnipotent, and omnipresence. That's why we need a God who is all-knowing, a God who has all power, and is everywhere at the same time. All we have to do is believe in Him, and all His promises and rewards will be granted to us. But we must be obedient to His will. Yes, I added something else: being obedient to His will. All our lives, we have been obedient to something, or someone, whether it's good for us or not, like the battered wife who stays with her husband for years because of the kids, or the addict who gets a drink, or a fix as soon as they get up in the morning. We go through these things, and we are obedient to them, so why can't we be obedient to His word that will bring us life everlasting and lead us safely from this evil place? We surrender to things from the outside that don't do us any good, so why not try something new and surrender to God? It will bring you peace and joy without buying something new.

By being obedient to His Word and serving Him, we have the opportunity to experience unbelievable joy. I must say, everyone who thinks that they've got this is only fooling themselves. Our ultimate goal is to be like Jesus, which we strive to do, but we come up short. You see, the beauty is in striving to reach the goal of being 100 percent like Jesus. When you have the opportunity to help someone, or give food to a neighbor down the street, ask yourself, "What would Jesus do?" You know He is all loving and all giving. You are on your way to being that way too.

It's not easy being a real Christian once you are saved. Here is what most of the churchgoers do: They sit down in the congregation and do nothing but go to church. Most members don't even pick up a hand and help. There is so much work to do, but they don't even pick up their Bibles. They stop growing. And when someone new comes into the church, they don't know how to welcome them. So in a lot of cases, the newcomer doesn't come back. In other words, they become a blessing blocker. God didn't save you to sit down and just take up space. If you are going to do nothing, then let someone who is struggling to get your seat have it. When God blesses you to be saved, He wants you to go out and save others. If not, you will be less in the Kingdom of God.

It is selfish and an injustice to have something so good and not share it, and there is punishment to those who do this. It is worse to know what you are supposed to do and not do it than to not know. As our Maker and our Creator, God gave us a manual that teaches us how to live a peaceful wholesome life, that teaches us how to treat our fellow man, and have a secure, joyful, and fulfilled life. This manual is called the Bible.

I think we can all agree with this example: When we purchase a car, television, or another type of appliance, there is a manual and warranty that comes with the new purchase. The manual explains how to use the product safely and properly. The warranty protects the product due to any breakdown within a certain time period, usually two or three years. In addition, we can often purchase an extended warranty for another four or five years. Some manufacturers give a better warranty than others, so as consumers, we compare who has the best plan. A smart buyer knows that the company who gives the best plan has, in most cases, the best product. Some car companies give a one-hundred-thousand-mile warranty coverage on the transmission and engine, whereas another company only gives a fifty-thousand-mile warranty coverage. It is more than likely that the car with the warranty that covers more mileage is the smarter purchase, especially if everything else is equal.

You trust and believe that the car manufacturer is giving you all the details on how to operate the car, yet you hardly ever pull the manual out of the glove compartment unless there is some trouble with your vehicle. The car manual is very important to the vehicle. It tells you when to get an oil change, it gives you all the information you need to maintain the vehicle, and it explains the warranty in full detail. It even gives you information on how to contact the maker of the vehicle if you have any problems that you can't figure out. There is nothing the manual doesn't cover. On top of that, your vehicle's dealership is available to assist you at your convenience and repair what's covered in the warranty. Often, if you register your car with the automaker, they will even extend the warranty.

When we are feeling low, or when the world seems to be against us, when our life is in shambles, when sickness comes in, when we are broken down mentally, physically, and spiritually, God gives us His manual to fix what is wrong in our lives. He has churches around the world that can repair our broken-down bodies and get us back on the path of righteousness. If we contact our Maker, He can give us an extended warranty—an abundant life. Some of us know where to go when our being is broken down, but as soon as we get it repaired, we return to the activities that turned our lives into a shambles. If we want our lives to get better, we have to read the manual and follow the instructions.

The Bible teaches us how to live a righteous life in this society. It instructs us on how to get along with each other, how to treat each other, and how to be upright people. Our manufacturer is an all-knowing God who loves us very much. He wants all of us to have a relationship with Him. He is not going to force us to come to Him. He wants us to come on our own. That's why so many of us choose not to come to Him but to do what we want to do. It feels good to do as we choose until what we are choosing turns bad, and we are sinking into quicksand, looking for a hand to pull us out.

At some point in our lives, we have all asked God to rescue us. Very often, once we were out of trouble, we got right back into it, only to call on God again. We did not realize that it was God who saved us the first time. We thought one of our friends rescued us and didn't even think to thank God. How must it feel to save someone's life and not even get a thank you? How ungrateful that must seem. But He forgives us because He knows that a lot of us don't understand what is really at stake here. We have no idea that we are treading in deep waters.

Jesus commissioned His disciples to carry His Word to the four corners of the earth to make sure that everyone gets a chance to hear His Word. Remember faith comes by hearing the Word, so we must get the Word out. Everyone is having some kind of movement from gay rights to #MeToo. Cases are being taken to the Supreme Court, and new laws are being put on the books. I can safely say that the church fire has been going out for the last twenty to thirty years, but if the church would start a movement, we would get many more souls to advance into the kingdom.

If the gay rights movement is asking for anything, it is to be recognized in society and given equal rights. That's it. They don't want to be outcasts. And now the Supreme Court says they legally belong and have all the rights and privileges as everyone else in America. The church has to move in this new direction. Things have changed in our society. Now I'm not saying that the church has to change. The Word of God is the same yesterday, today, and forever more. If the church changes to accommodate this new world, we will dilute the Word of God and make it weak. Remember God says do not add, or take away a Word. If we believe that, we must act like we do. We must always remember that if we draw closer to Him, He will grow closer to us.

We can't forget why we were saved. It does not matter how long we have been in the church. If it's been twenty years or thirty years, and we don't get it until now, it's okay as long as we go out now and do what we were saved by God to do. We know that to who much is given, much is required, so it's time to roll up our sleeves and do what God said of His will. Remember, if we don't do it, He will find someone who will. Do not pass me by, gentle Savior. We should be worthy of His calling.

Let's not wait until we are bogged down with life's woes and worries until we are sinking in quicksand to call on God. Let's seek God before we are drowning, before life throws us a curveball, so we will have the power of God to soften the blow. Momma and Daddy can't help us because they need help too. This is bigger than us and our family. The Bible helps us in our relationships, with our jobs, and with our grown kids who have gone astray. It helps us deal with every aspect of our lives. This is why God inspired people born thousands of years apart to share His Word. He wants to help us live happy and wholesome lives among each other.

In society today, something has to have a cost attached to it in order for it to be of any value. If something is free, it does not seem to interest people. If God's Word was not free and instead cost a whole lot of money, we would be madly fighting over His Word to keep it among our own set of people. God designed it so that the poor would have access to the manual as well as the very rich. Nobody can say they cannot afford the Word. The book is given away, yet no one wants it. It costs nothing, yet most people don't own it. The people who do own the manual don't take the time to read and study it in order to live better lives. God is standing at the door and knocking. He is waiting for us to let Him come into our hearts to get our lives in order. All we have to do is believe in Him and get to know Him.

PEACE

I would like to introduce you to a spirit called peace. Peace will never exist in an atmosphere of chaos, confusion, calamity, hate, envy, or jealousy. Its light will be snuffed out if we hold onto resentment toward another person. Resentment can be triggered by something as little as someone saying, "I don't like your dress," or "I don't like your shoes." We may hold onto resentments for years. Every time we see someone we resent, we may frown, or treat them differently, even though they may not remember what they said, or did to make us dislike them. This can go on for years and even decades.

This is especially true when someone goes on to the other life, especially if they were the head of the household. Once they are gone, the peace that was in that family is gone too. Siblings start going after each other, like they hate each other with a passion. In most cases, it is about who got the house, or who got the most money, the jewelry, or the car. They fall out, and in some cases, they never speak to each other again over something trivial. After a while, they forget what got them to the point of hating their brother, or sister. It runs deep in the soul and mind over and over, and the hate gets bigger and bigger until they are feeding on pure hate. I have seen people who are still holding onto resentments from high school over something that was said, or done to them often by their best friend. It was never resolved, and they are still holding onto resentment in their forties. Resentment can hold us down and change who we are.

Here is how you can get peace from that long and drawn-out situation. If you are holding a resentment, go to the person you have resentment toward and let them know why you feel that way. I tell you, the peace that will come over you is unbelievable. All it takes is for you to be the bigger person. I know your first thought is *I'm not going to them. They have to come to me.* Remember they are not the one who has been harboring these feelings all these years. You have to take the first step, and the sooner you do, the sooner you will enjoy the peace that comes from letting go and letting God into your heart to act on it. Try it, and you will immediately feel a sense of peace come over you.

Have you ever had a friend who didn't like someone for whatever reason, and even though you didn't know that person, you started to dislike them too? It could have started with something as little as your friend walking by that person and saying hi and the other person not hearing them. From that point on, your friend started to carry a resentment. It's just that easy to start to hate, to have hate take over your life. You start to become a hateful person, and no one wants to be around you. If hate enters your heart, it will show in your personality. You have to understand that there are some people who wake up in the morning with hate and malice on their minds. They want to hurt someone. They love to start arguments and fights, and they want to inflict pain on others for no reason. This is what makes them happy, to set some quicksand in an innocent person's life and watch them go under.

Remember the bully on the playground who was always trying to keep people living in fear, whether by taking their lunch money, starting fights, or pulling a little girl's hair. If you encountered a bully on the playground when you were a kid, they were often bigger and older than you and made you afraid to go to school, yet you never told your parents, or the teacher. You were too afraid. Bullies don't feel good until they make someone else's life miserable. They have to inflict pain on someone in order to feel good about themselves.

Then you have the people who love to wake up worrying about something. They worry about not feeling well, they worry about bills, and they worry about their friends. They have to worry. This is their morning fix. The difference between bullies and worriers is the worriers inflict pain on themselves, and the bullies inflict pain on others. Neither will ever be able to get peace.

We have to look into our lives to find out if we are the worrier, or the bully and then work on changing our behavior in order to become better people. It is important to change bad behavior before we have children because children see what we do instead of listening to what we say. We don't want to pass our bad behavior down to the next generation. It has to stop, and why not let it stop with you? Why don't you become the trendsetter? Yes, it takes courage, but you have the power to make the change. Do it to save your lineage. Condemn hatred, prejudice, and bullying in your family. It is a curse that has been lingering for too long, and if you don't step up to the plate, who will? You have the opportunity to stop hate right in its tracks. There is too much of it going around, and it's wasted energy that can be used toward something more positive. Once you let a little peace in, it will run through your family, like yeast runs through dough. Those of you who bake know about the effect that yeast has on dough, how it feeds and expands the dough, turning it into bread.

Peace and quiet can take a little getting used to, even if we yearn for it. Humans are creatures of habit. Once we get used to doing something, it settles in our spirit and becomes a habit. Once something becomes a habit, we have to have it every day. For example, I met a couple from New York City who could not fall asleep unless they heard the outside traffic and car horns blowing. If it was too quiet, they would toss and turn all night long. People who live in the country need it to be dark and quiet in order to fall asleep. Any little noise wakens them. Let's use babies as another example. If babies are put to sleep in a quiet environment, they will waken at the slightest sound. On the other hand, if the TV is on every time a baby is put to sleep, the baby won't be able to sleep without some kind of noise. The early years in our lives are very important. A lot of our experiences will stick with us our whole lives.

Let's come back to you who has the power to make a change. You have the power right here and now to pass this on to your family and friends. You have the influence to do it because your family and friends look up to you with your new life. They will make changes in their lives by watching you. It would be an injustice to your family and friends if you squander the power you hold in your hands. Once you have found peace, you must start to plant it everywhere you go.

Then look around to see the peace grow where you planted it. It's a beautiful thing to see God's work in the land of the living.

This is how peace works. Say you need a thousand dollars, and you ask each of your ten thousand followers on Facebook to give you ten cents. This is a small amount,. That's how peace works in your hands. If you give a little to the ones you know, they won't even know that you planted it in their lives. Remember the example of the yeast: Just a few ounces will run through ten pounds of dough. You don't have to try to figure it out. It just happens like that in God's hands. All you have to do is plant peace everywhere you go, and it will grow into every facet of your life. Everyone you come into contact with will get a whiff of its scent, and they will take it to their families and so on.

When we get used to peace, we will never exchange it for arguing, or chaos. These types of behaviors become very gross, and we will refuse to have them in our lives. Peace makes the soul healthy. Yes, peace can help heal the body. Have you ever come home to a quiet house? Oh, how peaceful that can be. Your mind is at peace when your environment is peaceful. Trust me, there is no better feeling than having your mind at ease, not having to worry about anything. Have you ever felt that? Well, now you can, and it doesn't cost anything. It is a gift to us from God. This is just one of the many blessings that He has for those who come to Him.

To acquire peace, we have to change what has been a curse for our families. Don't even think about wiggling out of what you need to do to make your family better. You have been chosen to act on behalf of your family. When you see wrong, you can't just stand there and ignore it anymore. Be courageous and plant the seed of peace in your family. All you have to do is plant it. Don't do anything else God will take it from there.

When a farmer has his seeds on the table, preparing to plant them in the ground, he makes sure to keep the carrot seeds separate from the corn seeds so that when he starts to plant, the corn is not growing with the carrots. That's all he has to do. He can't do anything else for the seed. If he tried to do anything else, he would interfere with nature. God takes over once the seed is planted. He waters it and shines the sun on it, and the seed bears fruit that we can consume. So you just plant the seeds of peace, and let God take care of the rest.

Can you imagine what a farmer goes through while he is waiting for his seeds to sprout? He hopes and prays for a good harvest that all his hard work will come to fruition. When you plant good seeds—a little peace here, a little patience and kindness there—they may take time to sprout. A seed starts by spreading roots down into the ground where the eye can't see. After a while, a bud protrudes out of the ground, and you can start to see the seedling grow. This is how God works in you. You might not see a change at first because the growth starts on the inside. You have to become grounded in the Word so that you can withstand the storms of life.

Becoming saved doesn't mean that you won't go through any storms. As a matter of fact, you are going to be tried at the beginning more than ever (I will explain that later), so you have to be prepared. The good thing is the Father will be with you, and He will never give you more than you can bear at one time. He allows these storms to happen so that you can start to develop and rely on your inner strength. Don't put your focus on the storm. Put your focus on God. He has put the storm under your thumb to be squashed. Once you accept God into your heart, then greater is He that is in you than what is in the world. You will be able to overcome anything through God.

Go ahead and promote peace and see how it works on your behalf. Start to replace hate and envy with God's love, peace, joy, kindness, and patience. While you are refining those attributes within yourself, start to plant the seeds in others so that they can reap a harvest too. God will see to the growth in other people's hearts. Your job is to plant the seeds, stand back, and watch them grow. There is no better feeling than seeing a newcomer, green behind the ears, grow in God, and do God's will to save other souls. The only thing that comes close to it is when our children turn out well as adults, as parents teaching our grandchildren. You feel proud that you played a part in shaping their lives. On the other hand, seeing your children grow up to be troublemakers hurts the heart very deeply, and it should because it reflects on you in a sense. But remember you can't take all the blame. Your children will have to be accountable for their actions the same as you are accountable for yours.

Know that whatever point you are at in your life—young, or old—this is the time that God intended for you to allow Him to come into your heart and prepare you to go on the battlefield and start saving souls. You must let your light shine. Do not be ashamed of God, and He won't be ashamed of you. Proclaim Him to the mountains and claim Him wherever you go. When you do this, do it with gentleness and kindness so that you don't startle the souls that you are going to help save. Remember how you were at the beginning—timid and fragile. All you have to do is bring the Word. God has already done the rest. God tells you to dress up for the battle and then go to the battlefield, but He fights the battle because it is not yours. It's His. You have to show up to see God show out.

I think it is safe to say that your life is getting a little better by now. You have God in your life, and you are exercising your inner attributes. You are on the right path. You are getting to know God for yourself instead of having someone telling you about Him. You are beginning to see blessings in your life that you cannot explain. Do not try to understand, just enjoy your newfound life and help others along the way. The more you help somebody, the better you will feel. It is true that it is better to give than to receive. Just a short time ago, we were looking for happiness in all the wrong places. Now we are bubbling on the inside with it. Continue to promote peace and may peace come to reside in your earthly tent.

TRUST

When a man and a woman join hands in matrimony, they vow to love, honor, and cherish one another, but trust is what really holds a marriage together. You would think that love would be the main ingredient, but people fall out of love and still stay married. You see, mutual respect will keep a marriage intact. Kindness toward each other will keep it intact. But if you lose trust, there is no recovery. Trust is imperative in a relationship. In a friendship, trust has to be established first, not love. We grow to love a person, and we can grow out of love, but trust is totally different from love. For example, police officers have to trust their partners with their lives so that they don't have to think twice when they are out on the streets. They learn how to work as a team, and they are both on one accord to protect and serve. Believe this, if an officer breaks this trust with his partner, no one else will want to work with him. He will always be that guy who broke the trust. When trust has been broken, it cannot be put back together again.

In the military, men and women go through basic training together. In addition to undergoing rigorous physical training, they must get to know their comrades and learn to trust them. When two soldiers are in a manhole together, and the enemy is approaching, they trust each other with their lives. There can't be a stronger trust than that—to trust your fellow man with your life.

The relationship we have with our parents is the building block on which we begin to trust. As infants, we are not coordinated enough to move our arms and legs, so we trust our parents to feed us when we are hungry. We trust them to clean us up and put warm clothes on our limp bodies, to change our diapers when they become soiled. We begin to see this trust when we start to cry, and they come to our rescue. When they hold us with their strong arms, we trust they won't drop us.

As babies, we are totally dependent on our parents. We can't walk, we can't talk, and we can't feed ourselves. The only thing we can do is sleep and cry and poop, so we need our parents for everything. When we get to be a few months old, we learn how to handle the bottle. How good our first taste of independence feels! And then we drop the bottle and go back to depending on our parents. Before long, though, we can grasp and hold on to that bottle for dear life. Then comes one of the most fearful times in our lives, our first steps on wobbly legs. "You want me to get over there by myself? Mom and Dad, you should not do me like that. You don't love me, or you would continue to carry me, but since it makes you happy to see me try to walk, I will keep trying." Sooner or later, the day comes when we are able to let go of Mommy's fingers while we are walking. "Look, Mommy and Daddy. I'm walking on my own! I can get around by myself."

I could go on to the bicycle and the training wheels, but I'm sure you get the picture by now.

So we build this gigantic trust in our parents. As we grow up, our parents look like giants in our eyes. They provide for our every need. Whatever we ask for, they either get for us, or work on getting it. They never seem to let us down. As we get older, we meet our teachers and build a trust with them that they will teach us how to spell, how to count, and how to get along with our classmates. We trust the priest, or preacher who leads our church. We learn to trust friends. Sometimes it takes years to trust someone in a relationship. Trust is something where we have to give everybody the benefit of the doubt. It is the only way a relationship can work. We are not going to be around people we can't trust, and when trust is broken, it can't be built again.

There was a man who worked at a Fortune 500 company who had worked his way up the corporate ladder and became vice president. He had a lot of pull and power in the company, and he was highly respected in the community and in the church. He had a family, and while his son was still in college, he told him that he would have a position in his company as soon as he graduated. He promised his son that he would hold that position, especially for him. Sadly, right around the time the son was getting ready for graduation, the father passed away, and his promise was never fulfilled.

There was a boy and girl who met in their first year of high school. It was love at first sight. They did everything together. When you saw the one, you saw the other. They were inseparable. They really grew to love one another. When they graduated from high school, they went to the same university and graduated at the same time, still dating one another. They trusted each other without reservation. They loved each other so deeply that they got married. It was a marriage made in heaven, as they say. The husband got a job and was making good money, and they began to have children, three in all. Life was going well. They never had much trouble, only the normal ups and downs that go on in a family. Mom and Dad were happy together.

One day, in their fifteenth year of marriage, the husband, Jack, called his wife to let her know that he and some of the boys were going out for a few drinks after work, and they had a designated driver, so she didn't have to wait up. After a few hours, the guys were feeling the effects of the alcohol. Some ladies joined them, and they were laughing and playing pool and drinking. Jack was having the time of his life. One of the women took an interest in Jack. She was about ten years younger. Jack was around thirty-five, and she was twenty-four. They began to talk, and it turns out they had graduated from the same university. They had so much in common that Jack could not believe it. The woman and her girlfriends were out celebrating her new job. She had no boyfriend, neither did she have any kids. She was like a breath of fresh air. Jack could see freedom in her, and he was attracted to her, and she was attracted to him because he was an older man and well-established. As it got later, they agreed to go someplace quieter, so they left the bar, grabbed a cab, and went to a hotel.

They began to have an affair. When Jack's wife found out about the affair, she was very hurt at the thought of her husband being with another woman. The pain she felt was overwhelming, and she could not shake it. She tried and tried to get it out of her heart, but she could not. She was a virgin when she met her husband in their first year of high school. She thought about how she consummated her marriage to him. She loved him and still loved him after the affair, but the trust was broken. Every time he left the house to go to work, or to the corner store, she wondered if he was still in contact with that other woman.

We have to understand that as humans, we are not perfect. Not to excuse Jack's behavior, but human beings are fallible. What we say and do doesn't always come out right. That's why we have trial and error. We can promise someone the world, but we can't always back it up. This is not the case with God. We can count on God to back up His promises. He has never lied to us, and He will never forsake us. He loves us more than anything. He gave His only begotten son to die so that we could have eternal life with Him. All we have to do is surrender to Him and serve Him.

How do you serve Him and do His will? You start by trusting Him. You are no longer dependent on your parents for everything. You can stand on your own two feet. But you are not in the safe comfort of your parents' home, trusting in them to protect you from harm's way. You are out in the big world, and you don't know what the next second will bring, but God knows everything. He knows the beginning and the end. He is the one our parents were depending on while we were trusting our parents. We thought all good things were coming from them, when in reality, it was God blessing them. If you want to feel the same security, love, and happiness you felt as a child, turn to God. He covers us in His wings of love. All we have to do is depend on Him and trust Him, like we did our parents, and He will do a thousand times better than our parents could ever have done. If you give Him your all, He will bless you abundantly. You will be blessed, and your children will be blessed.

God has promises that He will give you, and you do not have to worry that they will not be fulfilled. He is Alpha and Omega. He has never broken a promise. We know this from our ancestors who wrote His promises on scrolls and on the walls and mouths of caves, on clay tablets that they buried in the ground. They knew that God has promises, blessings, and rewards waiting for us if we serve Him. Remember the man who promised his son that he had a special job for him and then he passed away before he could fulfill his promise. Well, that won't happen with God. He is the beginning and the end of time. He doesn't send a promise out that will not be fulfilled. No one can change what God puts out in the atmosphere. You can trust Him with your life. He will never ever let you down. "'For I know the plans I have for you,' declares the Lord. 'Plans to prosper you and not harm you, plans to give you hope and a future.'" God promises to be with us until the end of the world, and in all these years, He has never lied, or said something that didn't come to pass. We have our ancestors to verify that.

You don't have to try to understand at this point. It's not necessary. Just trust the Spirit to lead you. I can tell the Spirit is guiding me when I do something that I don't normally do—when I offer to help someone, or give someone a kind word out of the blue, when I call someone I haven't seen in a long time and tell them I love them, when I step outside myself to do something kind for a senior citizen, or visit a sick friend in the hospital. You will know when the Spirit is leading you. Ask Him to lead you, and He will hear you. He will make it happen. Trust Him, and you will have no problems in your life that are too big. You have a Father who can take all the water on planet earth, hold it in the palm of His hand, and not a drop will fall. He knows your future. Why go to anyone else to know what lies ahead in your life? He has the answer to everything you want to know. He will give you insight into your future. Draw near to Him, and He will draw near to you. You have to trust in what He says He will do to those who come near to Him.

A lot of our decisions are faulty because we don't know the outcome. We can't see the end result of our decisions and that makes us more prone to mishap. God knows and sees the end of all our paths. If we are in a relationship with Him, we can go to Him who is all-knowing. We can't put all our trust in our friends. That wouldn't be fair to them. They don't have the power to save us because they need to be saved too. Before we come to the way, we are in darkness, stumbling along in our lives. We have to come to someone who is in the light and is getting to know God who can lead us along so we can get closer to the light. That's more than enough to start to understand that all this starts with just a little ounce of yeast.

To trust, we start out with just a mustard seed of faith. We don't start out with 100 percent of faith, or trust. We just have to plant the seed in our hearts, and it will begin to grow. We might not see it right away but then one day, someone will say, "I see a change in you." We still might not see it, but just keep pressing toward the mark of His higher calling. We will begin to teach others who are just arriving to Christianity. God is everything we are looking for in our family and friends. He is loving, kind, and compassionate to our needs. He will treat us better than we treat ourselves. He is protective, gentle, and forgiving. He is merciful. I don't know of any place, or anyone I can go to and get all this. There is no one who can promise these things and keep their promises. With Him, I am never alone, or lonely. He is always in the midst, ready to wrap me in His wings of love, like my mother did when I was a baby. Once I saw the light, my life became better. Of course, there are hardships. Everything does not always go my way, but God always seems to soften the blow. As our knowledge grows in God, I pray that He will reveal himself to us and that our trust will grow in Him so that He will show His will and give us the courage to carry it out.

HOPE

Hope is an expectation, a desire, a feeling that something good will happen for us. We don't see it, but we hope for it to happen. If we don't have any hope in our lives, life is not worth living. That's how important it is to us. Just imagine if you woke up every day without hope. Stop for a minute and think about having no hope. It's hard to imagine waking up every day and not planning, or thinking of a future, not wanting to achieve anything, or have anything. It's sad to say, but there are people in this world who have no hope. Some people have fallen on hard times. Some people had homes until they lost their jobs, and their last resort was to go to a shelter to regroup and not be a burden on family members. While they are in this situation, all they think about is having their own home again. That's what motivates them to get it together—to have their hope come to fruition.

With that said, there are two kinds of hope. A lot of people live on negative hope, like entering the Publishers Clearing House sweepstakes, or playing the lottery. When the lottery is at a hundred million dollars, they line up to play their numbers and start planning what they will do with all the money. This occupies their minds all day long. They want to win so much that they promise if they hit, they will take care of the poor and give money to their families. They think about this until the numbers come out, and once again, they have different numbers. Day after day, year after year, they hope and pray to win, only to be let down again and again. They give the lottery god all their hope, and it never delivers them from their dim situation. In fact, it puts them deeper in the hole because all their hard-earned money has gone down the drain, never to be recovered. It's a vicious cycle, a merry-go-round that never stops. I have to wonder what makes them think they will help the poor if they win the lottery. They could have helped the poor when they were going to the lottery machine every day. Money doesn't give us character, or morals.

Another name for negative hope is false hope. There is not much difference between the person who has no hope and the person who has false hope. There are so many ways that you can get caught up in false hope, and it really does have us believing that we will get the prize. It's easier to catch a bird flying in midair by jumping from the ground than it is to hit the lottery. We have to get away from negative hope, erase it from our minds. I could give you many more examples of false hope, but I think you get the idea.

Before we move on to positive hope, let's understand one thing: The world does not owe you a thing. If you think it does, you will always be at a disadvantage. You will feel like you don't have to do anything to make your life better. There are people who work hard every day. They go to work, they save their money, and they buy things for their families to survive. But if you are hopeless, if you believe the world owes you, and if you think you don't have to work, you will stay in need. The only way you can overcome this is to find God. While you are in shallow waters, don't go out into the deep waters where you are not able to tread water. You will drown in all your miseries. There is hope. You just have to learn how to tap into it. Thank God the Father is waiting for the hopeless. He will bring comfort to your soul so that you can get up from the cold sidewalk, so you can come out of the homeless shelter, and so you can stop putting money into the lottery machine that never gives back dividends.

False hope boils down to fear of life. Want a good life? Start putting your hope in God. He can bring your hope to fruition so you can see it and touch it. Hope comes the instant you believe. You can challenge me on this, but if you try, you will see with your own eyes that what I have said is true. I didn't know hope existed until I received Jesus in my heart. I now see the world with a new set of eyes. I believe that God wants the best for me. I can feel it in my soul.

Hope makes you feel alive and gives you something to look forward to, whether it's watching your kids become successful, or your grandkids playing in the backyard, or having a healthy newborn. Hope is healing to the heart. It will get you up in the morning and give you a reason to live. Hope is believing that no matter what kind of situation you have gotten yourself into, God is going to work it out. Whether it turns out in your favor or not, He will be with you, and you will have better days ahead. You can bank on it.

Prayer and hope go hand in hand. You must pray about what you want. It is not hard to do. You just go somewhere quiet and talk to God. He knows what you want before you even ask for it. As long as what you are hoping for is not selfish, or harmful to another, pray about it and watch how God brings it into the physical world.

Positive hope will give you the strength to do things that you never thought possible. A pregnant woman from a third-world country will walk thousands of miles to America, risking her life and the life of her unborn child for the hope of a better life. Can you imagine the joy that she will feel when she steps onto American soil after walking so many miles and facing every danger known to man? If you have no hope, find it and live life as it was meant for you to live. Remember that any step you make toward God will be one less step for your kids to make. You are not getting to know God just for yourself. You are doing it for your kid's sake because you will share what you have experienced. The Word says start children off on the way they should go, and even when they are old, they will not turn from it. This is one of God's promises to those who serve Him.

The God that you are putting your hope is a God whose hands have gathered up the wind, who can wrap up the waters in a cloak, and I am not talking about a glass of water but about the oceans, the seas, the lakes, the ponds, and the swimming pools. He has His hand in the spiritual and the physical realms. He who has established the ends of the world, who can counsel Him? Who does He owe? Who is over Him? Your hope will not be in vain.

Sometimes we don't know what to hope, or pray about. Sometimes we pray for something, and once we get it, we pray to have it removed. It's so much easier to give it to God and leave it in His hands and let Him fix it. I know it's hard, but you can't go wrong. He knows all. It's a process. Do it little by little and that way, you can gain trust in Him. Eventually, you will put it all in His hands and not have a worry on earth. You can put your kids in His hands, your problems in His hands, and your relationships in His hands. Put it all in His hands and live free. But don't forget to do the footwork. You can't hope for a job but then stay in bed every morning just hoping. This is false hope. You have to get out, like that pregnant woman from the third-world country. What if she had just hoped and not put any effort toward her hope? She would still be where she was, and her baby would not have been born in America. We must not get comfortable with the norm and stay in a state of poverty. God wants more for us. We have to grasp hope, hold on to it, and make our lives and our children's lives better. Even in a state of hopelessness, we can find hope. All it takes is to place hope in God. "I know the plans I have for you," declares the Lord. Plans to prosper you and not to harm you, plans to give you hope and a future."

LOVE

Love is a word that is the topic of many conversations and is often misunderstood. We can all remember our first love. The first time I fell in love, I was nine years old. I was convinced that we were going to get married. I would get butterflies in my stomach every time I saw her. She was the apple of my eye. She made me so happy. I could not get her out of my mind. I would think about her day and night. She was in my homeroom class, and I would carry her books home from school. In those days, that's how people could tell who was boyfriend and girlfriend. Our relationship ended when I moved to another state. I was so sad. My heart felt like it was coming out of my body. That was my first experience with love, or should I call it kiddy love?

Love is innocent when we are kids. When we become teenager, we look at love much differently. Now we have the parent's car, and we take our girlfriend to the movies and go places so our love can grow a little more serious. We become a little more intimate. We love our parents, our siblings, our cousins, and our friends, so we've become very familiar with love. We have all this love going around, and we feel that we are knowledgeable about this thing called love, but some of us have a misconception about what love really is.

Let's say you meet a man and fall in love with him. You put him on a high pedestal and place high expectations on him. You expect him to make you happy and make you feel better when you're feeling low. He makes you feel safe and secure. He is your everything. You love him more than anything in the world, and you can't live without him. You decide to marry and move in together. Before long though, your real selves come out, and you start seeing things that you didn't see at the beginning, things you don't like. Your love starts to dissipate. You fall out of love, and the two of you break up. Once again, you feel heart broken, like you did when you were younger.

Love is not just a feeling. It's an action. Love is the joining of two hearts as one. Love means you love someone else the same way you love yourself. Love is knowing a person's faults and loving them anyway. Love is never jealous, or envious. Love is not pumped up. Love is trust. Love means that when your partner gets sick, you are there by their side. Love means staying together and working things out when you fall on bad times, or have some bumps in your relationship. Love is keeping open communication no matter what. Love is not going to bed mad at one another. Love is forgiveness. Love is not trying to change your mate into who you want them to be but loving them for who they are.

There are different degrees of love. When we are growing up, we love our parents and siblings. We may argue with our siblings, or get mad at them, and Mom and Pop may have to break up a few fights, but our love for each other usually overrides any angry feelings before too much time has passed. Sometimes we grow apart from our siblings when we go off to college, or start families of our own.

The love we feel when we fall in love with someone is a different kind of love than the love we have for our parents and siblings. When we get married, our love for our spouse grows deeper. We love them more intensely. It's not the same love we had for our families when we were children. When we have our own families, we do the same thing our parents did. We protect them and make sure that they are secure by providing them with clothing, food, and shelter. Remember, love is more than just a feeling. Love is also an action. In addition to feeling love for our families, we show them love by taking care of them. This is what love is.

A parent has immeasurable love for their children. Parents love their kids so much that they would rather pass before their children do. They would do anything for them. They would even die so that their children can live. As a parent, would you give one of your children up for this cruel world? In other words, would you end one of your children's lives? Would you give your only son up for this world? You don't have to answer that question. Of course, you wouldn't.

God loves us so much that He gave us His only begotten Son. His son had no children, He was the last of the line, and yet He allowed us to kill His Son so that we could be saved. What exactly does the word saved mean to a Christian? Saved means to have eternal life. See, He gave His Son's life for our lives. His Son was sacrificed for all our sins so that we would come closer to God. If we believe in Him and His Son, we can receive life in the here and after. Yes, I mention the after. The spirits that dwell in our bodies will live after the here is gone. The Son of God has already been born of the resurrection. He was the first to be born in the new life that we will be going to when we pass from this earth. Jesus told the people who were on the earth in His time that He would go to prepare a place for all of us, meaning everyone born since the beginning of human existence on earth. This is a number that cannot be counted, but God knows the number. He knows everything about you, whether you know Him or not. You see, it does not matter if you don't know Him because He still exists, but it would be better for you to know Him, or get to know Him in order to have a better life here on earth.

Do you know anyone who would forgive all your sins, turn an eye on your shortcomings, and still love you no matter what you did wrong? Someone who can give you confidence when you're feeling low. Someone you can always count on. I do, and His name is Jesus. He has never, and I mean never, let me down, or disappointed me. Oh, what a God I serve! I put all my trust in Him because He has the power to make everything all right. He can make a promise to me, and if I don't see the promise, He will give it to my kids. Do you know anybody who can do that?

God gives us three things we can count on: rewards, blessings, and promises. These are His guarantees. All the world offers us is vanities, lotteries, casinos, makeup to make us look younger, shoes to make us taller, lifestyles of the rich and famous, and hype that's not attainable for the average person. In God's house, we are all equal. God loves us all the same, whether we are rich, or poor, Black, or White. For those who serve and worship Him, He has a little more favor. All it takes is an ounce of His favor to make a difference in our lives.

You see, God is love. God's love is forgiving, not puffed up, not wayward. He is always the same and never changes, for God is the same yesterday, today, and forevermore. You can learn about Him, and you don't have to worry about anything changing. It will never change, whereas people change every day. A friend can promise you something, and if you don't act the way they think you should, they will welch on the promise. It's probably happened to you, or you have probably done it to someone else. That's all right. You didn't know. You are new to the way, and your old way of thinking will begin to change. From this point forward, your mind will be renewed. Your heart will change for the better. You will grow in God's love.

Love is doing things for people without expecting something in return. When you love someone, it covers a multitude of wrongs. For example, if your kids do something wrong, the love you have for them will always cover their wrong. I have seen mothers visit their adult children on death row because they loved them despite the crime they had committed. This is how strong a mother's love is. Love is powerful. Love could conquer the world if it was used more freely. If we had more real love in this world, we would not have any wars. We would be able to iron out our differences, forgive, and move on without killing. Love can change the impossible into the possible.

We must understand that when we get saved, we still have work to do. We have to work on our bad behavior. We have to let go of our bad habits. If we ask God to help us, it will be a lot easier, but a lot of times, we don't. It is easier to work on these things at the beginning of our newfound life. Otherwise, they will follow us in our Christian walk, and we will be a Christian with a lot of problems. Nothing good in this world comes easy, or else everyone would have it. So don't rush the process. Remember the farmer who planted the seeds. He must wait patiently for them to grow. After a few days, he may check to see if anything is growing and not see a single seedling. He might go back a week later and still not see any signs of growth. The plant has to grow roots in order to receive water to sustain it, and only then will it protrude above the surface. God works the same way in us. He blesses us to plant the Word. If we don't see any results, we must keep watching. We can't get discouraged. We are being rooted in the Word the same way the seeds the farmer planted are being rooted in the ground. The happiness he feels when he sees his harvest is overwhelming. We will be just as happy when we see ours. Glory be to God for His love endures forever.

Let's talk a little more about the farmer. In this day and age, no one has as much patience as the farmer. He realizes more than anyone that God's work is real. Once the farmer plants his seeds, he prays for God's rain and for God's sun to shine. Harvest depends solely on God's work in the land of the living. He depends on God's resources to live. If he has a few years of poor harvests, he will go out of business. We have seeds to plant, just like the farmer. We are planting the Word of God into people who don't know Him. Just like the farmer, we hope for a great harvest. And just like the farmer, we have to be patient and trust that the seeds that were planted in us and those that we plant in others will take root and outwardly begin to blossom, like a beautiful flower.

I asked some seniors and teenagers to tell me about love. Some said love means having strong, or unconditional feelings for a mate and providing protection and security for your mate. Others said love means caring for your mate and your children more than yourself. A fourteen-year-old girl, who looked to be a little fragile and quiet, told me that love is something that you don't have to question. I must say I didn't expect the answer she gave. It was like an arrow piercing my heart. This is the way it is with God. You don't have to question His love. You just know that He loves you. He wakes us up every day, and we have to thank Him for the new grace and mercy He gives us each day He wakes us.

With God's blessing, I'm able to use my limbs. I'm able to walk, shower myself, go to work, and put food on my table. These things and more have been granted to me from a loving God. If we take a step toward Him, He will take a step toward us. His love is everlasting. Trust in Him. He has been proven. Read the history books. Everything He has said has come to pass. Some people died before God's promises came to pass, but we know those promises were fulfilled from their sons and daughters who knew what God had promised and saw it come to fruition. His Word has been proven over and over again. It's been recorded for thousands upon thousands of years and preserved in clay and on scrolls that our ancestors buried in the earth. Archeologists continue to look for artifacts all around the world that will help us understand our history. This is why books are so important. If we don't know about history, how can we know who we are, or where we come from? God loves us so much that He has given us a book to live by. The Bible gives us teachings and instructions on how to live a righteous life and how to love one another. It shouldn't be so hard. Imagine how beautiful the world would be if we could love one another as easily as we hate.

How can we turn things around? Teach your children to love instead of hate. Search your heart. You know what is good and what is bad. You know it's not right to be prejudiced toward people who are not the same color, or same ethnicity, even if your parents taught you otherwise. Why not be courageous today and make a decision to change what has been in your family for generations? Start teaching your children to love. Be a trendsetter. Reverse the trend so hate can stop with you. Sometimes it is hard to do the right thing, but you are stepping up. You are walking down a newfound path that you never stepped foot on. You are at the fork in the road. One way is a path that you have always walked; the other is your newfound life. The choice is yours. You have a compass inside of you that will lead you to the right way. It takes a lot of courage to change your life for something you are unfamiliar with, but others have done it, and you can too. God is love, and He wants us to spread the love that we have all over this earth. Remember, you have the power. Use your power to make sure that one day down the line, your children can say you taught them how to love.

Hate is evil. Hate is contagious. It is a spirit that gets on the inside and runs all through our bones and never do we question it. Hate is deceptive. It is sad to say that we have way more hate in the world than love. Hate is easy to pick up and carry from one person to another. It spreads like the bubonic plague.

How can a nation of people with different religions hate others who don't worship the same way so much that they commit genocide? They kill thousands, or even millions of people based on the beliefs handed down from their parents who got them from their parents and so on. Hate gets into the crevasses of our hearts, and we pass this hate on to our innocent children.

Hate came into our existence when Cain hated his brother, Abel, for being more righteous. God favored Abel's offering over Cain's, and this caused hate to fester in Cain's heart so much that he killed his brother. Take a look in your heart and replace the hate that is festering there with God's love. The change begins right there in your heart. You see, this is the only way, we will be able to rid this plague from our society. Love can conquer all. We just have to love instead of hate. Remember you have the power. You just have to learn how to use it.

To stop this plague called hate that is cursing our kids and our communities, we must go to the source. God is love, and we have to start there. We have to start teaching our little ones about love, then in one or two generations, depending on God's will, we will be able to see love run through the world, like a wildflower. There will be no more wars, countries will be able to lay down their arms, people will start to treat others the same as they want to be treated, and we will love God with all our hearts. We will pick up his manual and learn how to treat our fellow man and give to those who are needy and struggling instead of violating them because they worship another way.

It is not up to us to bring wrath down upon other people. That's God's job. He is the one who is going to judge. What's so funny is that these people think they are doing what God wants them to do. We know enough about God to know that He is all love. Why would He do something like that when He is the one who made all of us? That's like saying that a parent raises two boys to grow up to fight each other to the death. God is not crazy, so we should not make God out to be what we think He is. God is all love, and to carry out His wishes is to love one another, not to kill one another. He is our Father. He blew breath in us, giving us our first gasp of air. We might not see the change once we start teaching it to our little ones, but all we have to do is plant the seed, and God will do the rest. It's the same concept as the farmers. They plant the seed, and the rest God will do.

A seed is just a seed. If it sits on your table, it will stay a seed. It's not until you dig up a little earth and put the seed in the dirt and cover it up that it will begin to germinate. It's the same metaphor with our Lord Jesus. He was murdered and put into the ground for three days. After that, the power of the Father lifted Him up and brought Him back to life. He was the first to be born of the resurrection. He rose to be on the right hand of God, and He is now interceding for us. At the appointed time, He will return to get those who have believed in Him.

    Let's not forget. God so loved the world that He gave His only begotten son so that we shall live. To the newcomer, this is the most important part of your Christianity. You have to believe that God's existence is real. You have to confess with your mouth that Jesus Christ is Lord and Savior and that he died for you and believe in your heart that the Father raised him to sit on the right hand side of him, and you will be saved. You may not feel any differently, but this does not mean that you are not saved. No human can tell you whether you are saved or not just because they felt one way, and you did not. Only the Father takes care of that part. That's his job, not the seasoned saint. Learn to hear the Word but also go home and read it for yourself. Remember there are some people out there who think that they are doing a job for God when they are doing a job for man. That's why we have so many wars. They are listening to a man's selfish ideas, someone who has sold his ideas to a body of people who get behind the movement without questioning why. If they could answer why, you wouldn't believe what comes out of their mouths. God is love, and if your actions don't reflect that, then they do not come from God. But God forgives us because we know not what we are doing. God loves the good and the bad. To all the people in the world, I can say in my heart that I love you in spite of the wrong that you are doing. I know that before it is over, love will conquer all.

Epilogue

Now that you have let God into your heart, it is important that you learn all you can about Him. This is one of the first things you must do. You have to read the Bible. To be honest, it can be a little boring at first, but as you continue to read and get acquainted with His Word, it will become marrow to your bones, healing to your body, serenity to your mind, and medication to what ails you. It will heighten your awareness. Mostly everyone can remember when they first got saved.

As you experience the benefits of the new path that you have embarked on, you will also have some bumps in the road. Things are going to come up that are going to try to deter you from your path. You must not allow this to happen. If you follow these distractions, you will be taken off course. It can take a lifetime to get to where you are right now. You may suddenly become too busy to get with like-minded people, or start working a lot of overtime, whereas before you got saved, you didn't even have a job. The kids are going to become more demanding. All kinds of things are going to crop up to take you away from God. But if you endure, just imagine the rewards that will be waiting for you! You have the power to handle all the distractions—go to work, bear the children. God won't put more on you than you can handle on any given day. He promises us that.

Do you know that a rubber band has to be stretched every so often? If it stays in its form without being stretched, it will become weak, and when you go to wrap something together with it, it will pop. It's all right for us to be stretched a little. This is what keeps us on our toes. They used to say in the old days that it is good to step outside your comfort zone. In fact, learn to be comfortable in your discomfort. This will help you become stronger. Forget how much pain you had to go through before you started calling on God. There are many ways to get to God, but if you are like me, you took the bumpy road to get to this fork in your life. The path I was on could have been leading me to a dead-end street. I'm here now, I'm in, and I don't want to go back to what I knew. I may not have the opportunity to change my life and serve Him again.

You must know by now that this is not a haphazard predicament that you are in. This is real. Jesus said, "I am the way, the truth and the life. You cannot get to the Father but through me." Trust in God, and you can have the assurance that He will have your back. He will never leave you, or forsake you. Remember the promises He gave our ancestors are the same promises He has given to us because He is the same God yesterday, today, and forever. You only need to have faith the size of a mustard seed. The seed has already been planted in you. Let God water the seed with his Holy Spirit and let His Son into your heart and watch the blessings pour down on you from heaven. You will have so many blessings you won't have room for them all.

It's like this: You take your family to the ballpark, and you are having a great time, but your team is down one run. It's the last inning. Everyone knows that the guy at bat has a two hundred batting average. He has two strikes and three balls, and the opposing team has the best pitcher on the mound. The pitcher winds up, throws the ball, and the batter hits that ball straight out of the park. You jump out of your seat and release a sound, like a lion's roar. It is so unbelievable that the other team yells too. This is how it feels when you allow Jesus to come into your life—like hitting a home run when you're down one run with two strikes and three balls against you. It is just like joy bells ringing in your soul.

There aren't enough words for me to express what Jesus has done. You have to try Him for yourself. I challenge you to try Him. You will never, never go back to where you came from. You would do yourself an injustice to return to your old life once you immerse yourself in Him.

I was led to write this book. I feel a deep compassion for all my brothers and sisters on the earth no matter their color, or beliefs. Whatever our beliefs, they are not important unless they come with a spoonful of love toward one another, a spoonful of treating others as we want to be treated. This is how we will begin to get somewhere and learn to live among each other. We have to get a sharp knife and carve hate out of our society for good. We have wasted too much energy and money and lost too many lives because of hate. We have to look at our own lives before we force our will on others. We have to tear down the layers of hate embedded in our interior, and little by little, we can begin again as a nation. We may not see the change come to fruition, but we have the power right here and now to turn hate into love. We can't do this on our own—it would be impossible—but with God, all things are possible. There is nothing too big for Him to handle.

    I know there were times in my life that I didn't have time for God. I got caught in the trenches of life, and no one could save me. I was sinking in sin. But then I found Jesus, who I had been avoiding all my life. He picked me up out of the gutter, and I said, "Help me, Lord, and I will serve you for the rest of my life." You see, God can do the impossible. I was as broken as a cup in my mother's kitchen that had fallen off the shelf and broken into a thousand pieces. When a cup is broken that bad, there is nothing to do but to sweep it up and throw it in the trash. In the old days, mothers had cups that were only used for special occasions. Those special cups were stored in a cabinet nowhere close to the common cups. God took that shattered common cup that my mother would have tossed into the trash and put all the pieces back together. He put my life back in order and gave me a special task to do for Him. He loved me, even though I didn't know Him. He's a friend closer than a brother. He's my All and All.

    Amen.

INDEX

Page	Scripture	Verse
12	2nd Corinthians	5:17
15	Matthew	7:13
16	Hebrew	13:5
19	Proverb	3:5
22	Hebrew	13:8
27	Jeremiah	29:11
29	Ephesians	4:6
34	Matthew	7:13
37	Hebrews	12:5
38	Acts	1:8
39	Matthew	16:24
42	Ephesians	4:5
43	James	1:27
44	Psalm	119:105
46	Mark	4:21
47	Genesis	15:6
48	1st Corinthians	2:9
52	Matthews	18:3
56	Revelation	22:18
60	Galatians	5:9
67	Revelation	22:13

67	Ephesians	6:1
72	Proverb	22:6
76	John	14:1

Related Reference

Zondervan: New International Version

Old Testament

Genesis,	15:6
Genesis,	17:7
Deu	6:4
Psalms,	68:18
Proverbs,	3:5
Proverbs,	3:12
Proverbs,	18:21

New Testament

Matthew	7:13
Matthew	16:24
Matthew	22:37
Matthew	25:14
Mark	4:21
Mark	4:24
Luke	16:31
Luke	19:12–27
John	14:1
John	14:6

DEACON GREGORY HARRIS

John	14:25
John	14:26
John	15:16
Roman	10:7–9
Roman	12:2

New Testament

1st Corinthians	2:9
Corinthians	5:6
Corinthians	14:4
2nd Corinthians	12:9
Galatians	5:9
Galatians	5:16–22
Ephesians	1:4
Ephesians	4:4–7
Ephesians	6:1–2
Philippians	1:9
Philippians	1:29
1st Timothy	6:7
Hebrew	12:5
Hebrew	13:5–8
1st Peter	2:9
1st Peter	3:3

CPSIA information can be obtained
at www.ICGtesting.com
Printed in the USA
LVHW110529201021
700930LV00003B/300

9 781662 442162